by
Mary Ford

With step-by-step instructions

Published by Mary Ford Cake Artistry Centre Ltd.
28-30 Southbourne Grove, Southbourne, Bournemouth, Dorset, England BH6 3RA

Printed and bound in Great Britain by Purnell Book Production Ltd.

ISBN 0 946429 09 X

We stress the importance of all aspects of cake artistry, but always give special emphasis to the
basic ingredients and unreservedly recommend the use of 'Tate & Lyle' Icing Sugar.

CONTENTS

INTRODUCTION

This 120 page colourful and sumptiously produced book of children's celebration genoese sponge cakes, emulates the outstanding standards already set by Mary Ford in her best-selling step-by-step teaching and reference books on cake making, baking and decorating.

Each of the thirty-six cakes illustrated has been specially designed and prepared by Mary Ford for the book and every cake (excepting Rocky) is supported by the exact templates required to produce perfect 'cut-outs' from sugar paste – the prime decorating medium used in the book.

Eight pages of easy-to-follow basic instruction smoothly guide the cake-maker, whether housewife, mother, teacher or chef, through the preparatory stages of making, baking, filling and covering a sponge cake, on to the production of any one of the fabulous full colour designs.

As in Mary Ford's other publications, concise language and clear easy-to-follow photographs are prominent features. The cake-decorator has, as a result, an invaluable long-lasting 'work-horse' from which to produce super birthday and other celebratory cakes for boys and girls.

This is yet another outstanding instructional book in which Mary Ford can take justifiable pride and is, unquestionably, of excellent value.

S.+B.

PREFACE

Although hours of practice will improve performance, these decorated sponge cakes can be produced with just a little skill, patience, effort and planning. Reasonable care in following the straightforward and easy instructions in this book will, without exception, provide the birthday boy or girl with a superb celebration cake – to the delight of both the decorator and the child.

Our thanks go to all who have helped in any way whatever in the production of this book and, especially, to Stan and Betty Oddy.

Michael & Mary

THE AUTHORS

Mary Ford's lovable and unchanging rural English Bristolian character belies her tremendous success in, and impact on, the cake artistry world. Very obvious skills and ability make Mary a leader in her chosen profession and an international sugarcraft judge. Students of this beautiful craft come from all over the World to be trained in the Mary Ford School and her best- selling cake decorating books are referred to by all interested in cake icing skills.

Although only Mary's name appears in the title of this book, its production is the result of careful and harmonious joint endeavours by both Mary and her husband Michael. They shared the overall planning and stage-by-stage control of the book and, whilst Mary superbly decorated each cake, Michael skillfully and painstakingly photographed her work.

When 'relaxing', Michael enjoys the dangers of deep sea fishing and of 'investigating' far off places, whilst Mary looks forward to an annual winter's holiday in some very warm climate.

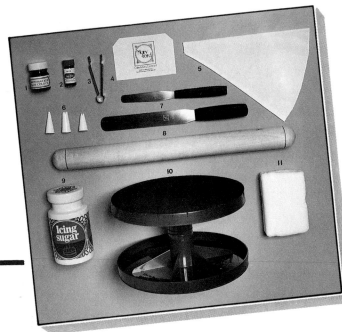

REFERENCE TABLE TO CAKE DESIGNS

PAGES	NAME	STYLE	SPONGE SIZES (inches)	CAKE BOARD SIZES (inches)	CAKE DOYLEY SIZES (inches)
12 – 14	**HAPPY**	PIG	5, 6, 8 round	11 round	12 round
15 – 17	**HENRY**	BOOK	8 square	12 square	–
18 – 20	**DORA**	DUCK	8 round	14 round	–
21 – 23	**CLIFFORD**	SNOOKER TABLE	10 square	12 square	12 square
24 – 26	**JULIA**	BUTTERFLY	8 round	12 round	12 round
27 – 29	**TERRY**	TRAIN	6, 6 square	11 square	–
30 – 32	**HEIDI**	COTTAGE	6, 6 square	12 square	–
33 – 35	**MACHO**	GORILLA	7 square	14 round	16 round
36 – 38	**MELINDA**	ORGAN	8 square	12 round	–
39 – 41	**JOE**	PRIZE CUP	7 square	12 × 14	–
42 – 44	**TRICIA**	HEART	7 heart	11 round	11 round
45 – 47	**BERNARD**	OWL	8 round	12 round	12 round
48 – 50	**ELLEN**	SCHOOL SATCHEL	8 square	15 round	16 round
51 – 53	**JIMMY**	RACING CAR	6, 6 square	14 square	–
54 – 56	**TRUDY**	CRINOLINE LADY	2 pint basin	11 round	12, 9 round
57 – 59	**BENNY**	ALARM CLOCK	8 round	12 round	12 round
60 – 62	**PRISCILLA**	FAN	8 square	14 round	14 round
63 – 65	**TOBY**	CALCULATOR	8 × 5	10 square	–
66 – 68	**GEMMA**	GUITAR	4, 5 round and 4 square	12 × 14	–
69 – 72	**NOAH**	ARK	8 square	14 round	–
73 – 75	**MICHELLE**	TELEVISION	6, 6, 6 square	12 round	12 round
76 – 78	**CHARLIE**	CLOWN	6 round, 6 square	15 round	15 round
79 – 81	**STACY**	TRAINERS	8 square	14 round	14 round
82 – 84	**KEITH**	AIR BALLOON	7 round, 4 square	12 × 14	–
85 – 87	**BARBIE**	BED	8 square	14 round	14 round
88 – 90	**JASON**	LINER	7, 7 square	14 square	–
91 – 93	**PENNY**	PIANO	8 square	12 square	12 square
94 – 96	**ANDY**	SPORTS CAP	2 pint basin	12 square	–
97 – 99	**MANDY**	CALENDAR	8 square	12 round	12 round
100 – 101	**ROCKY**	DRUM	8, 8 round	12 round	–
102 – 104	**SWEETIE**	PANDA 'T' SHIRT	8 square	14 round	14 round
105 – 107	**BARRY**	AEROPLANE	8 square	14 round	–
108 – 110	**COOKIE**	CHEF	6 round, 5 square	12 × 14	–
111 – 113	**SANDIE**	SPORTS BAG	8 square	12 round	12 round
114 – 116	**FREDDIE**	FISH	8 square	14 round	14 round
117 – 119	**FROSTIE**	SNOWMAN	4, 8 round	14 round	16 round

GENOESE SPONGE

10″ round or 9″ square

INGREDIENTS FOR BATTER

Butter	3ozs	85g	⅜ cup
Margarine	3ozs	85g	⅜ cup
Caster sugar	6ozs	170g	¾ cup
Eggs, fresh	6ozs	170g	¾ cup
Flour, self raising sieved	6ozs	170g	¾ cup
Total batter weight=	24ozs	680g	3 cups

NOTE:

For 4, 5, 6, 7, 8 and 11 inch round sponges, respectively use 2, 4, 6, 8, 12 and 32 ounces of batter.

For 4, 5, 6, 7 and 10 inch square sponges, respectively use 4, 6, 8, 12 and 32 ounces of batter.

For an 8″ × 5″ sponge, use 10 ounces of batter.

For a 2 pint basin, use 8 ounces of batter.

(All ingredients should be at room temperature – 65-70°F – when making the genoese sponge)

Method

1. Using the genoese tin base as a template, mark and then cut out a piece of greaseproof paper.
2. Use a pastry brush to grease inside the genoese tin with white fat.
3. Place the cut piece of greaseproof paper into the bottom of the tin and brush over with white fat.
4. Mix, then beat the butter and margarine together in a mixing bowl until soft and light.
5. Beat in the caster sugar to form a fluffy consistency.
6. Break an egg into a small basin before transferring it into the mixing bowl. Then thoroughly beat in a small amount of egg at a time until all the egg is used. (Repeat for each egg, to ensure bad doesn't mix with good).
7. Pour flour on to the mixture and gently fold in – being careful not to overmix.
8. Spoon mixture into the prepared tin and spread it evenly with a spatula.
9. Place the tin at the centre of a pre-heated oven and cook for 20 minutes (375°F/190°C/Gas Mark 5).
10. Then open oven door slowly and, if the genoese is

pale in colour, continue baking until it is golden brown. This is the time to draw fingers across the top (lightly pressing) and, if this action leaves indentations, continue baking. Repeat the test every 2-3 minutes until the top of the genoese springs back when touched.
11. Remove the genoese from the oven and leave to cool for five minutes.
12. Remove genoese from the tin and place it upside-down on greaseproof paper covered in caster sugar.
13. Upturn genoese and place it on a wire tray until cold.

Storage

Wrap genoese sponge in waxed paper and store in deep-freeze for up to six months. If not frozen, use within three days of cooking. If frozen, use within three days of defrosting.

Chocolate Genoese

Use the above ingredients BUT replace 1oz of flour with 1oz of cocoa powder. The same method of making the genoese applies.

ALBUMEN SOLUTION
INGREDIENTS

Pure albumen powder	1oz	26g	⅛ cup
Water	6ozs	170g	¾ cup

Method

1. Pour water into a bowl and stir whilst sprinkling in the dried albumen.
2. Thoroughly mix and then stir occasionally during the next hour.
3. Strain the mixture through a sieve or muslin and it is now ready for use.

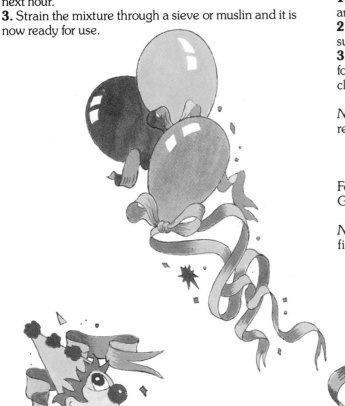

ROYAL ICING
INGREDIENTS

Fresh egg whites or albumen solution	3ozs	85g	⅜ cup
Sieved icing sugar or confectioners' sugar	16ozs	454g	3 cups

Method

1. Place albumen solution or fresh egg white in a bowl and stir.
2. Beat in ⅓rd of the icing sugar. Repeat until all icing sugar is used.
3. Beat mixture until light and fluffy and peaks can be formed. Scrape inside of bowl and cover with a damp cloth. Use when required.

NOTE: Separate fresh egg whites 24 hours before required.

SOFT ROYAL ICING

For soft cutting royal icing, add and mix 1 teaspoon of GLYCERINE to each pound of royal icing.

NOTE: Do not use glycerine for royal icing runouts and fine piping work.

SUGAR PASTE
INGREDIENTS

Sieved icing sugar	16ozs	454g	3½ cups
Egg white	1	1	1
Warm glucose	2ozs	57g	4tblspns

Method

1. Warm bowl containing glucose in a saucepan of hot water.
2. Sieve icing sugar into a mixing bowl and then add the egg white and warmed glucose. Mix thoroughly.
3. Knead the mixture to a pliable paste, then wrap in a polythene bag and store in a cool place.

BUTTERCREAM
INGREDIENTS

Butter	6ozs	170g	¾ cup
Sieved icing sugar	12ozs	341g	2 cups
Warm water – tblspns	3	3	3

Method

1. Soften butter and beat in a bowl until light.
2. Gradually add the sieved icing sugar (beating well after each addition).
3. Add and beat in the water (and colour and/or flavour if required).

1. Bake sponge of the size and shape stated under 'CAKE REQUIREMENTS' in the chosen cake design. Remove top crust, upturn and then remove bottom crust.

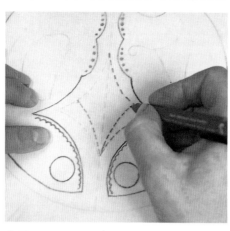

2. Trace orange design outline on to greaseproof paper from the template (in this instance the butterfly on page 26).

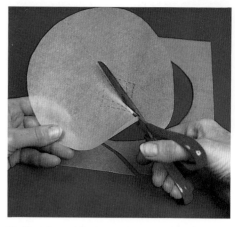

3. Cut shape from greaseproof paper template.

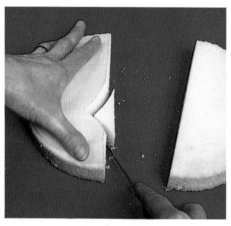

4. Place template on sponge and cut sponge to match the template.

5. Slice sponge and then fill with a preserve (jam) followed by buttercream. (To flavour and colour buttercream, see page 10).

6. When sponge is sandwiched, cover all over with a thin layer of buttercream and refrigerate for 30 minutes before covering with sugar paste.

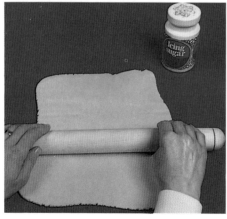

7. Roll out sufficient sugar paste on icing sugar to cover the sponge assembly. (To flavour and colour sugar paste, see page 10).

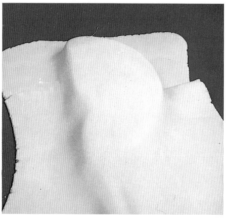

8. Place sugar paste over the sponge and fix by pressing lightly with the palm of the hand.

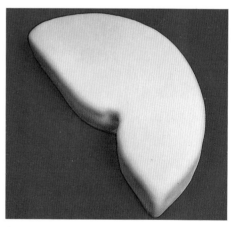

9. Trim off surplus sugar paste after ensuring all air bubbles have been removed.

STIPPLING BUTTERCREAM OR ROYAL ICING ★★★★★★★★★★★★★★★★★

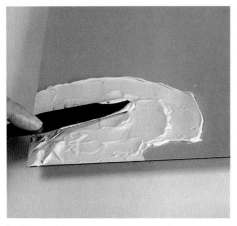 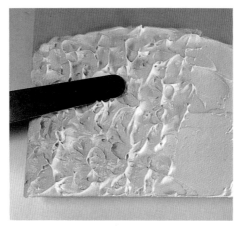 

1. Spread buttercream or royal icing on to the board with a palette knife.

2. To create a coarse stipple, repeatedly press and lift the palette knife into the buttercream/royal icing.

3. To create a fine stipple, repeatedly touch the surface of the buttercream/royal icing with a clean, dry, fine sponge.

CREATING SUGAR PASTE BUSHES ★★★★★★★★★★★★★★★★★★★★★★★★★★★

1. Press coloured sugar paste against the inside of a wire sieve, to form bush effect.

2. When of required size, cut the 'bush' from the sieve.

3. Decorate the bush with piped royal icing dots, to form flowers/berries.

PIPING A ROYAL ICING BOOTEE ★★★★★★★★★★★★★★★★★★★★★★★★★★★★

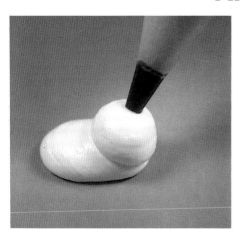  

1. Pipe a royal icing elongated bulb on waxed paper and then immediately pipe another bulb in the position shown.

2. Pipe a royal icing spiral line on top of the bulb.

3. Decorate the bootee with piped royal icing dots and a bow. Leave until dry.

★★★★★★★★★★★★★★★ FORMING AND FIXING A SUGAR PASTE FRILL ★★★★★★★★★★★★★★★★★

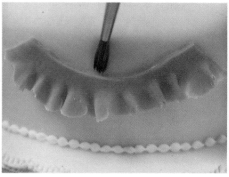

1. Roll out sugar paste (using cornflour for dusting). Cut sugar paste to the shape shown using cake cutters and a knife.

2. Roll a cocktail stick over the fluted edges to form the frill.

3. Fix the frill by dampening the upper edge (with a small clean paint brush) and pressing it lightly to the sugar pasted cake-side.

★★★★★★★★★★★★★★★★★★★★★★★★★★ CRIMPING SUGAR PASTE ★★★★★★★★★★★★★★★★★★★★★★★★★★

1. (This example shows how to crimp a pillow). Cover a piece of sponge with buttercream and then sugar paste.

2. Immediately squeeze top edge of sugar paste with crimpers (of the required shape and size).

3. Continue crimping until almost complete, then adjust the spacing to ensure there is an even pattern when complete.

★★★★★★★★★★★ COLOURING ROYAL ICING/SUGAR PASTE/BUTTERCREAM ★★★★★★★★★★★

Colouring Royal Icing

Colouring Sugar Paste

Flavouring/Colouring Buttercream

To avoid overcolouring, add colour to a small portion of royal icing and then stir in that portion to all the royal icing. Repeat the process until the required colour is obtained.

NOTE: It is not advisable to use blue colouring in royal icing, unless blue is the final colour required. Only approved edible colours should be used.

Dip a cocktail stick into the edible food colour of choice and wipe on to the paste. Then repeatedly fold the paste by hand until the colour is thoroughly mixed in.

Add artificial flavouring (or strained fruit, or zest of fruit, or melted chocolate) to the buttercream and then add a complimentary food colour and thoroughly mix. Be cautious not to overcolour.

NOTE: If mixture starts to curdle, immediately add more buttercream or icing sugar.

★★★★★★★★★★★★★★ MAKING A GREASEPROOF PAPER PIPING BAG ★★★★★★★★★★★★★★★★★

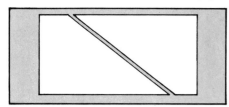 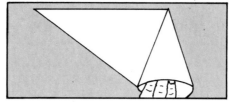 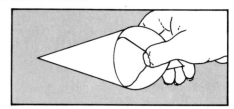

1. Cut a 12″ × 8″ sheet of greaseproof paper diagonally, as shown.

2. Position long side upwards and roll the paper in the manner shown.

3. Complete the cone shape and secure the open end pieces (with, for example, sticky tape).

★★★★★★★★★★★★★★★★★★★★★★★ PIPING A LINE WITH ROYAL ICING ★★★★★★★★★★★★★★★★★★★★★★

HOW TO PIPE A STRAIGHT LINE
1. To steady the tube, use both hands. Touch surface with tube end, keeping bag at the angle shown.

2. Squeeze bag until icing appears. Continuously pipe whilst lifting bag in the direction of the line to be piped.

3. Before reaching end of line, stop squeezing and lower the bag to the surface – whilst keeping line taut. Pull tube cleanly away.

HOW TO PIPE A CURVED LINE
4. To steady the tube, use both hands. Touch surface with tube end, keeping bag at the angle shown.

5. Squeeze bag until icing appears. Continuously pipe whilst lifting bag in the direction of the curved line to be piped.

6. Before reaching end of curved line, stop squeezing and lower bag to the surface – whilst keeping line taut. Pull tube cleanly away.

★★★★★★★★★★★★ HOW TO PIPE BUTTERCREAM / ROYAL ICING SHAPES ★★★★★★★★★★★★★

1. SHELL. Hold piping bag at the angle shown and start to press.

2. Continue pressing, whilst lifting bag.

3. Continue pressing until shell is of required size.

4. Stop pressing, then slide tube down along surface to form tail.

1. ROPE. Pipe spring-shape in clockwise direction, using even pressure and keeping bag horizontal.

2. Continue piping in a straight even pattern. Stop piping and pull bag away in a half-turn.

1. 'C' SCROLL. Pipe in clockwise direction, increasing the size of the circle to form the body.

2. Continue piping, reducing the size of the circles, then form the tail – using reduced pressure.

1. 'S' SCROLL. Hold piping bag at angle shown and start to press.

2. Continue piping in a clockwise direction, increasing the size of each circle to form the body.

3. Continue piping, reducing the size of the circles from the centre.

4. Continue piping and form the tail by reducing pressure.

HAPPY

Cake Requirements

5", 6" and 8" round sponges
11" round board
12" round doyley
Buttercream
Confectioners' dusting powder

Edible colours
Black – Brown – Red – Salmon Pink

Royal icing
Sugar paste

1. Slice and fill each sponge and then cover each with buttercream.

2. Cover each sponge with sugar paste and then mount as shown.

3. Mould pigs trotters from sugar paste, and fix.

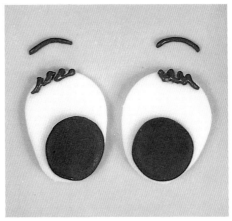

4. Cut and fix sugar paste eyes. Pipe eye lashes and eye brows.

5. Mould, cut and fix sugar paste snout and mouth. Pipe royal icing lines around mouth.

6. Mould, cut and fix sugar paste ears. Pipe royal icing hair.

7. Brush on edible dusting powder to give cheek blush. Pipe royal icing chin lines.

8. Mould and fix a sugar paste tail and pipe inscription of choice.

Before commencing any work on this page, please read the whole sequence of instructions and ensure the proper materials and equipment are to hand, as well as sufficient time to complete the cake. Additional information can be found on pages 4-11 (Index on page 120).

6"SPONGE

Fold

◄ 8" SPONGE

Fold

◄ 5" SPONGE

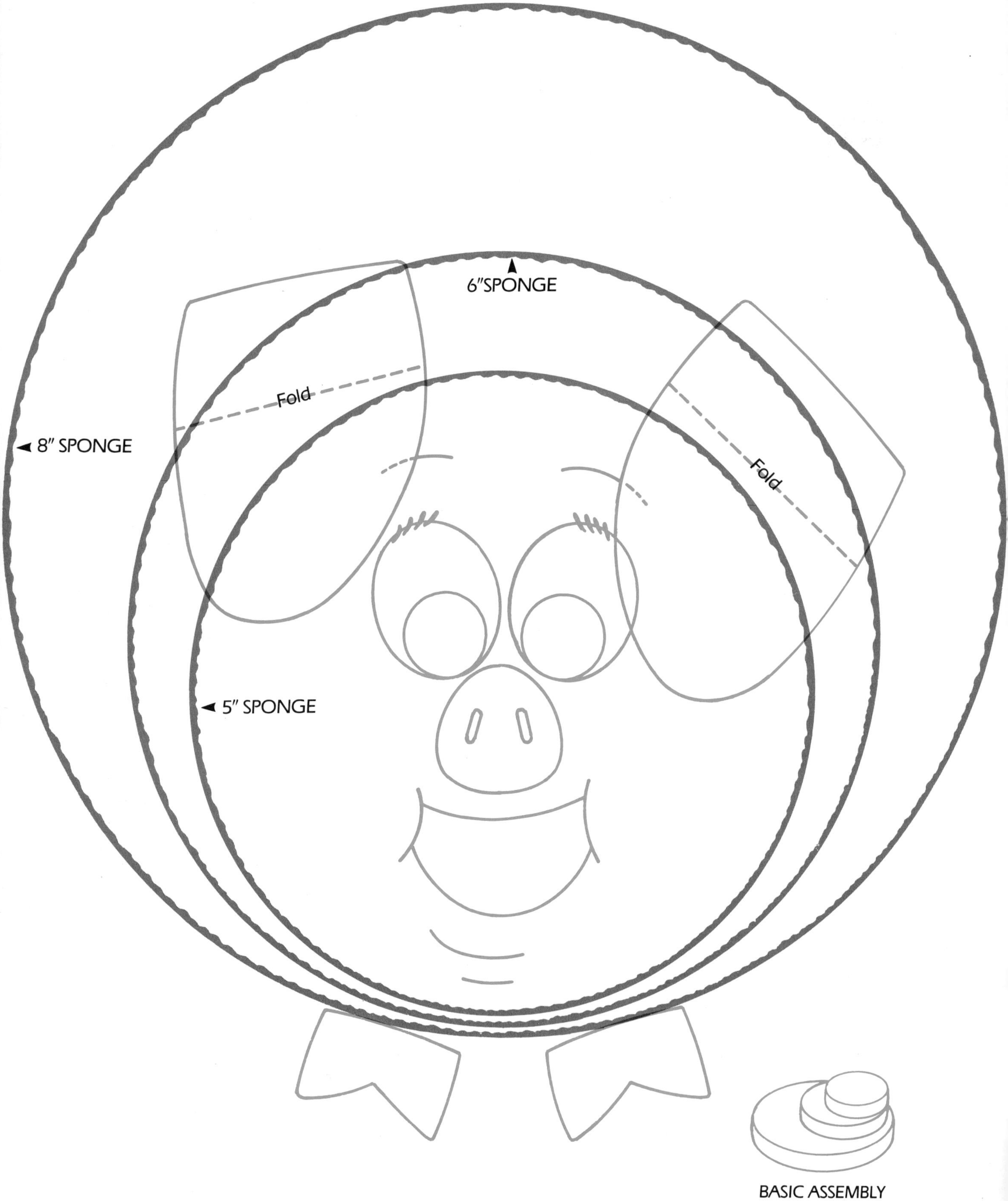

BASIC ASSEMBLY

HENRY

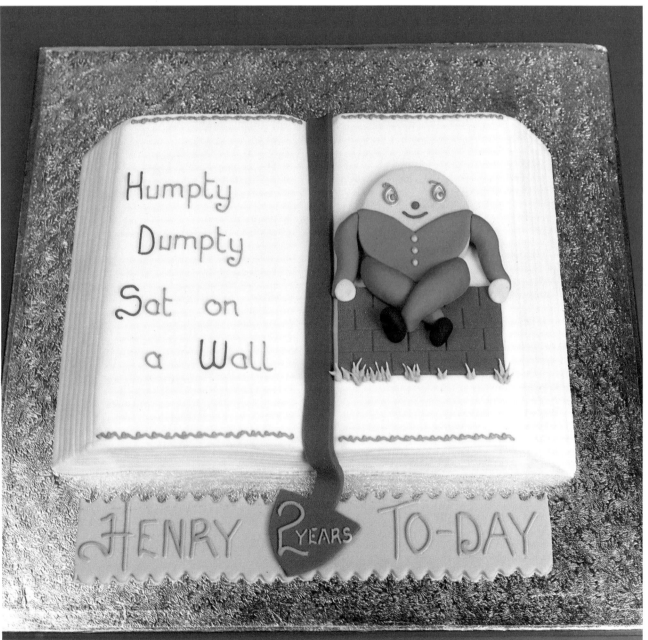

Cake Requirements

8″ square sponge
12″ square board
Buttercream

Edible colours
*Black – Brown – Christmas red –
Cream – Flesh – Green – Violet*

Royal icing
Sugar paste

1. Cut off end of sponge (using template as guide) and then slice end-piece diagonally, as shown.

2. Add one end-piece to each book-side, as shown. Cut and remove a "V" section from centre of book.

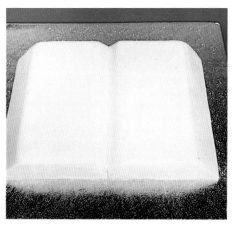

3. Slice and fill the book with buttercream and then cover with sugar paste. Place on board. Mark each edge of the book to form pages.

4. Make Humpty Dumpty's body and wall from sugar paste and fix to right side of book.

5. Cut, mould and fix sugar paste pieces to form clothes and hands. Pipe features, buttons and grass with royal icing.

6. Pipe first line of rhyme with royal icing on left side of book.

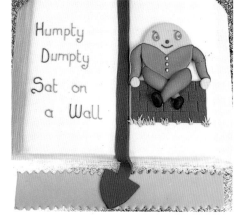

7. Make and fix – (a) a sugar paste plaque and (b) a sugar paste book-mark, as shown.

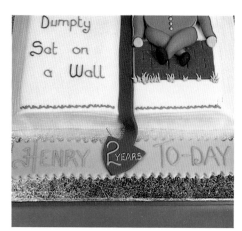

8. Pipe inscription of choice on to plaque and book-mark with royal icing, then pipe the lines shown.

Before commencing any work on this page, please read the whole sequence of instructions and ensure the proper materials and equipment are to hand, as well as sufficient time to complete the cake. Additional information can be found on pages 4-11 (Index on page 120).

Humpty

Dumpty

Sat on

a Wall

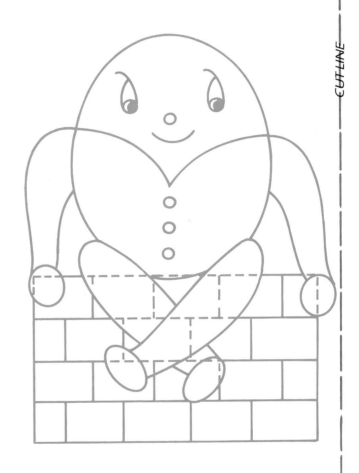

CUT LINE

8" SPONGE ▶

CUT LINE

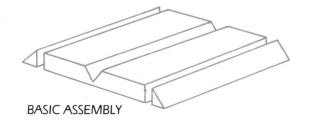

BASIC ASSEMBLY

END VIEW

DORA

Happy Birthday Dora

Cake Requirements

8″ round sponge
14″ round board
Buttercream

Edible colours
*Black – Blue – Brown – Christmas red
– Green – Raspberry – Yellow*

Royal icing
Sugar paste

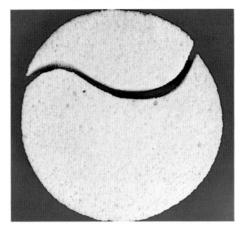

1. Cut sponge as shown (using template as guide).

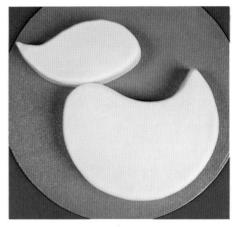

2. Upturn top section to form duck's head. Slice, fill and cover sponge with buttercream and then sugar paste. Position on board.

3. Pipe bill and eye with royal icing.

4. Pipe wing with royal icing.

5. Cut and fix sugar paste water and leaves, as shown.

6. Cut and fix further sugar paste leaves, as shown.

7. Cut and fix sugar paste flowers, as shown.

8. Cut, fix and decorate duck's handbag with inscription of choice.

Before commencing any work on this page, please read the whole sequence of instructions and ensure the proper materials and equipment are to hand, as well as sufficient time to complete the cake. Additional information can be found on pages 4-11 (Index on page 120).

HEAD

Trace pattern for head and turn over to assemble (see photo 2)

CUT LINE

◄ 8" SPONGE

WING

BAG

FLOWERS

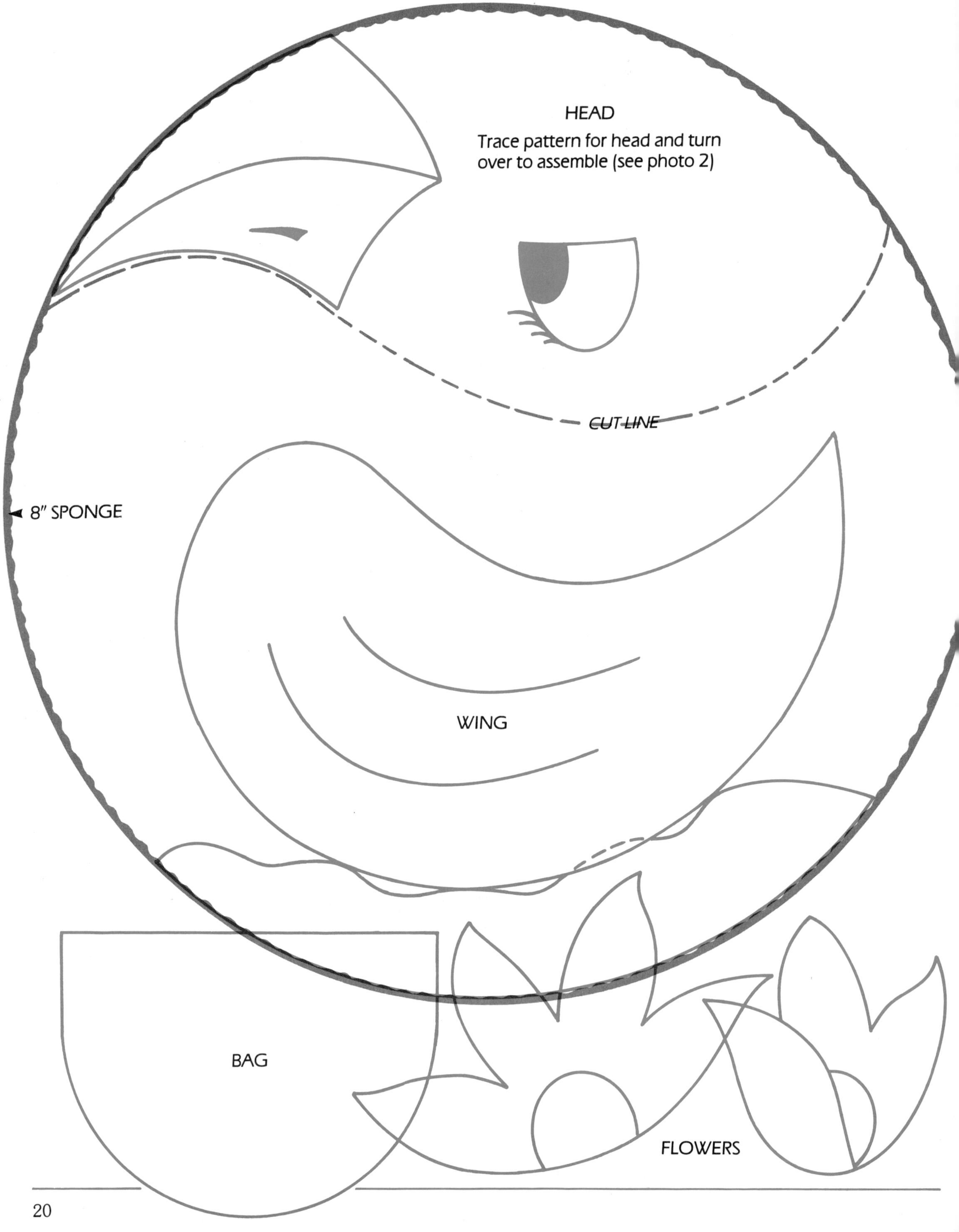

CLIFFORD

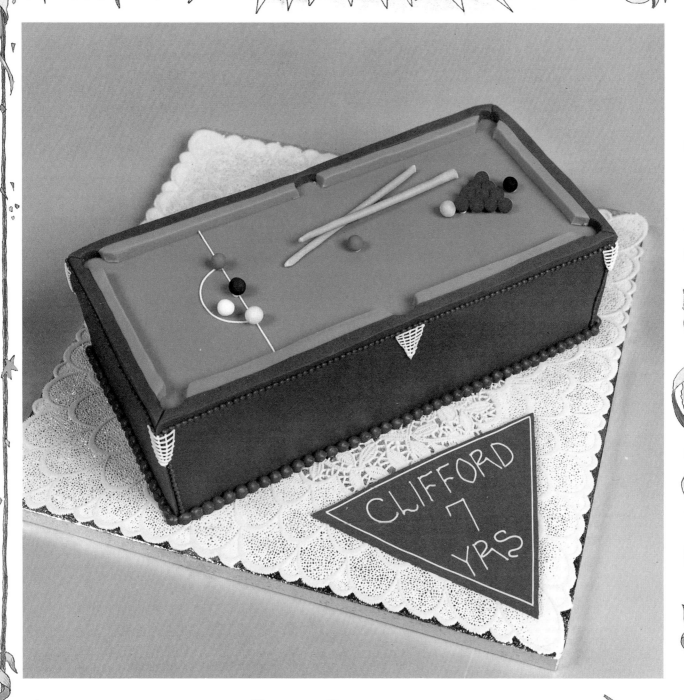

Cake Requirements

10″ square sponge
12″ square board
12″ square doyley
Buttercream

Edible colours
Black – Blue – Brown – Christmas red
– Cream – French pink – Green – Holly
green – Yellow

Royal icing
Sugar paste

1. Cut sponge in half. Sandwich, fill and cover with buttercream.

2. Cover snooker table top with green sugar paste, then cover sides with brown sugar paste. Place on doyley and board.

3. Roll out, cut and fix sugar paste edging to table top, as shown.

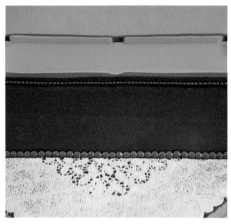

4. Pipe small shells with royal icing around the cake-base and the upper cake-side (to cover the sugar paste join).

5. Pipe table top lines and spots, as shown, with royal icing.

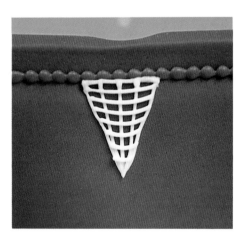

6. Pipe each pocket net with royal icing.

7. Cut and fix a red sugar paste triangle to the cake-board doyley. Pipe inscription of choice with royal icing.

8. Make and fix sugar paste snooker balls and cues, as shown.

Before commencing any work on this page, please read the whole sequence of instructions and ensure the proper materials and equipment are to hand, as well as sufficient time to complete the cake. Additional information can be found on pages 4-11 (Index on page 120).

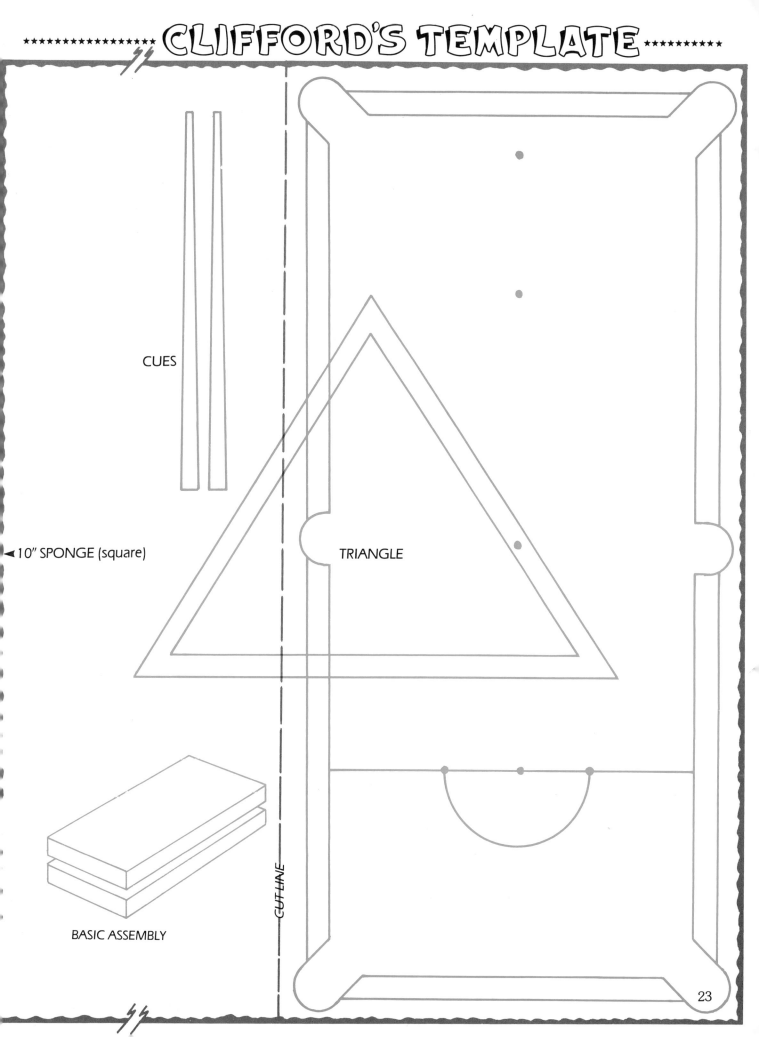

CUES

◄ 10" SPONGE (square)

TRIANGLE

BASIC ASSEMBLY

CUT LINE

JULIA

Cake Requirements

8″ round sponge
12″ round board
12″ round doyley
Buttercream

Edible colours
Black – Brown – Green – Peach – Violet – Yellow

Royal icing
Sugar paste

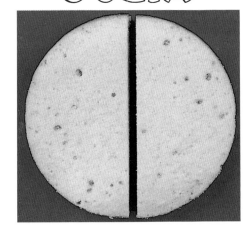

1. Cut sponge cake in half.

2. Reverse halves and cut to required shape (using template as a guide). Assemble parts to form butterfly.

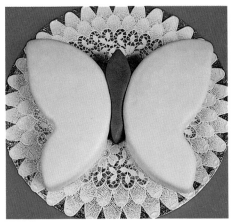

3. Slice and fill butterfly with buttercream and then cover with sugar paste. Place on doyley and board.

4. Pipe wing and body outlines with royal icing.

5. Cut and fix sugar paste discs to butterfly wings and then pipe eyes with royal icing.

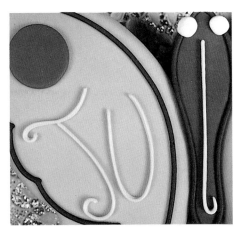

6. Pipe part of name of choice across wing and body with royal icing.

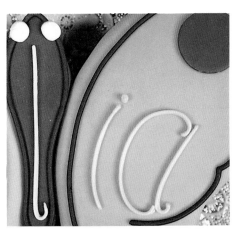

7. Pipe remaining part of name across other wing.

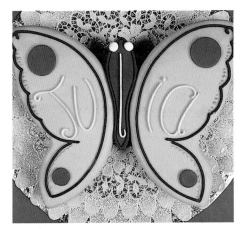

8. Decorate each wing with piped royal icing dots and curved lines. Place covered floristry wire into head to form antenna.

Before commencing any work on this page, please read the whole sequence of instructions and ensure the proper materials and equipment are to hand, as well as sufficient time to complete the cake. Additional information can be found on pages 4-11 (Index on page 120).

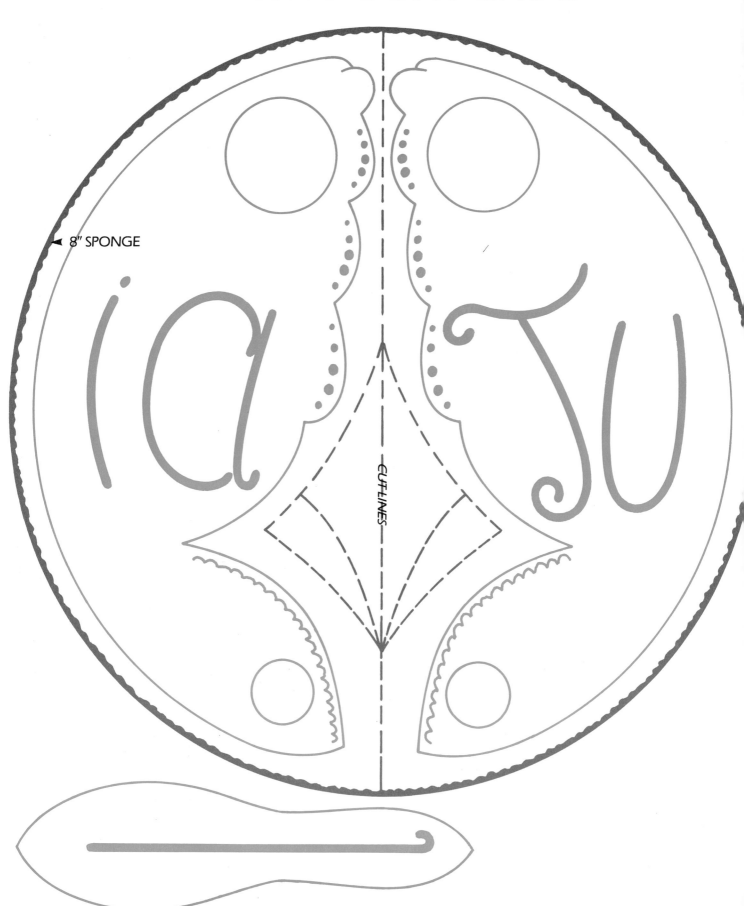

◄ 8" SPONGE

CUT LINES

TERRY

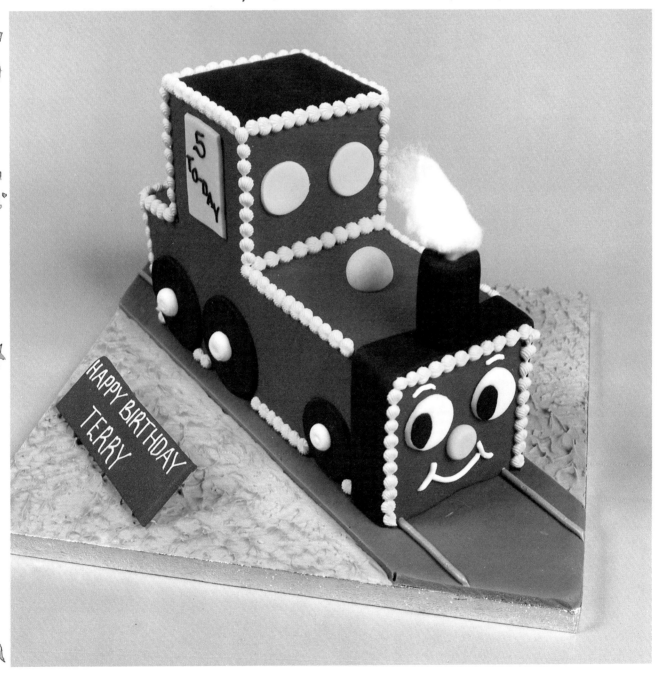

Cake Requirements

Two × 6″ square sponges
11″ square board
Buttercream

Edible colours
Black – Brown – Christmas red – Green – Yellow

Royal icing
Sugar paste

1. Cut and fix a sugar paste railroad across the cake-board. Stipple (see page 9) remainder of board with royal icing.

2. Place the two sponges together and cut off the quarter shown. Halve the quarter pieces and position at each end of the train.

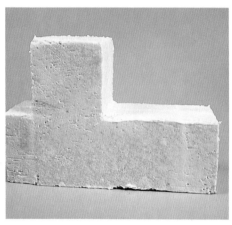

3. Sandwich, fill and cover the sponges with buttercream.

4. Cover train with red and black sugar paste, as shown. Place train on railroad.

5. Cut and fix sugar paste train wheels and pipe royal icing shells around the train's edges.

6. Cut and fix sugar paste eyes, nose, funnel and windows. Pipe face features with royal icing.

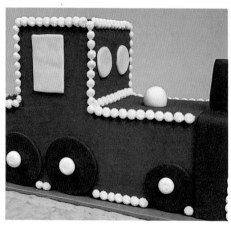

7. Cut and fix sugar paste whistle and windows. Pipe wheel centres with royal icing.

8. Cut and fix sugar paste plaque, as shown. Pipe royal icing tracks and decorate train and plaque as required.

Before commencing any work on this page, please read the whole sequence of instructions and ensure the proper materials and equipment are to hand, as well as sufficient time to complete the cake. Additional information can be found on pages 4-11 (Index on page 120).

TERRY'S TEMPLATE

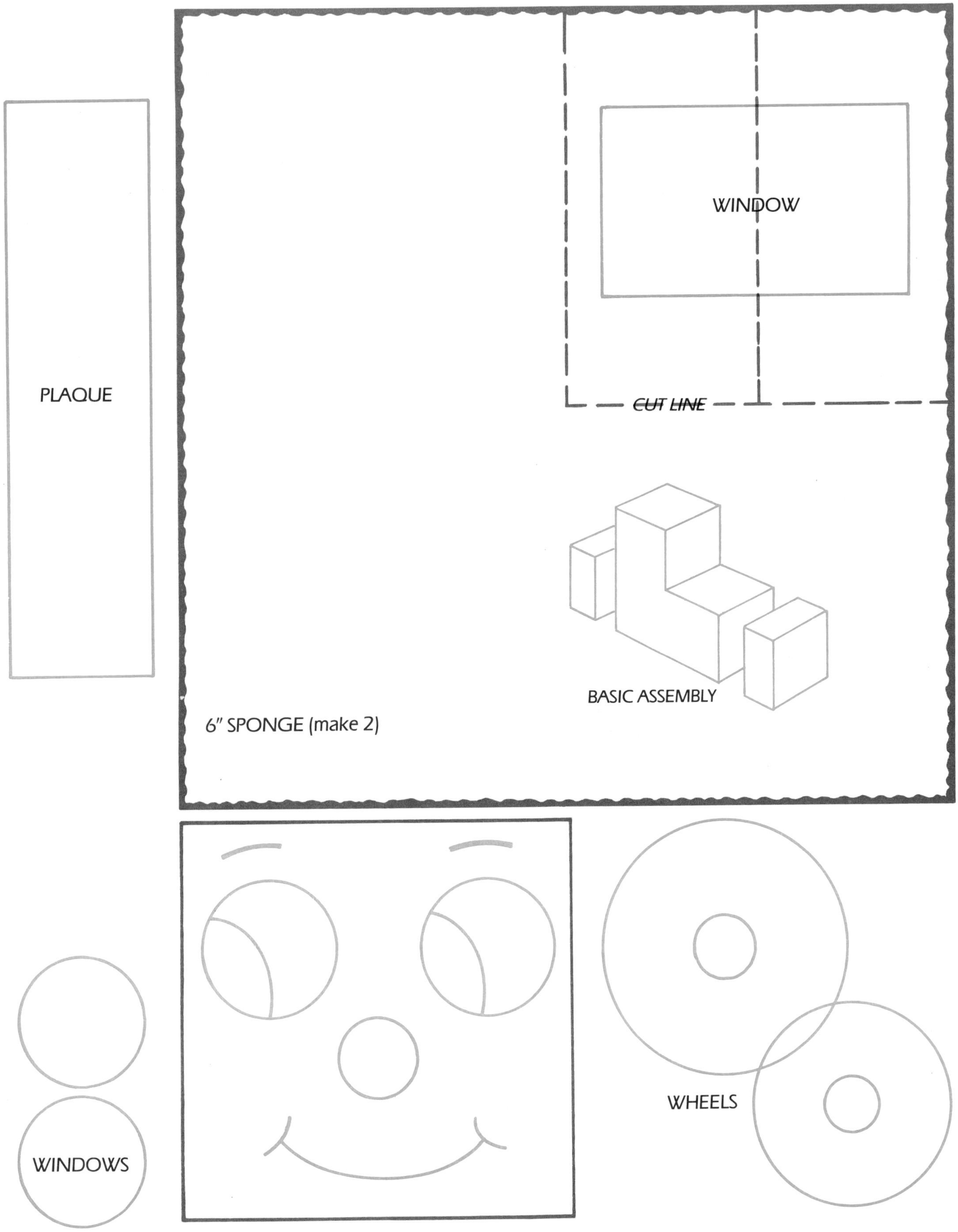
PLAQUE
WINDOW
CUT LINE
BASIC ASSEMBLY
6" SPONGE (make 2)
WINDOWS
WHEELS

HEIDI

Cake Requirements

Two × 6″ square sponges
12″ square board
Buttercream

Edible colours
Black – Blue – Brown – Cream – French pink – Green – Red

Royal icing
Sugar paste

1. Cut 2″ off each sponge. Sandwich the two large pieces. Cut an angle off one side of each remaining piece and assemble to form roof top.

2. Fill and cover the cottage with buttercream. Roll out, cut and fix sugar paste sides and roof windows, as shown. Place on board.

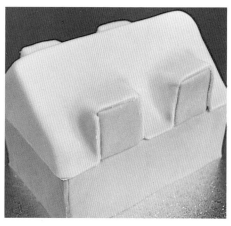

3. Roll out, cut and fix a sugar paste roof.

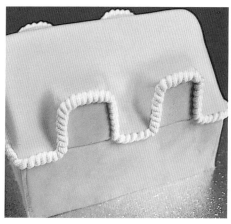

4. Pipe a royal icing rope line around the roof's edge.

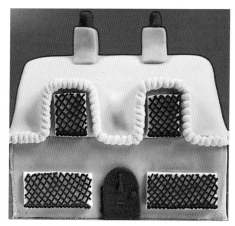

5. Roll out, cut and fix sugar paste doors, windows and chimneys. Decorate doors and windows with piped royal icing.

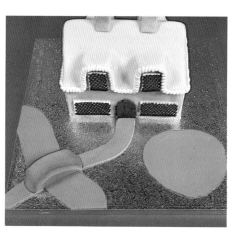

6. Roll out, cut and fix a sugar paste pond, stream, path and bridge.

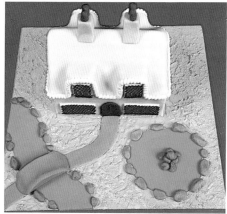

7. Stipple (*see* page 9) royal icing on board to form grass. Mould and fix sugar paste rocks, as shown.

8. Form, fix and decorate sugar paste bushes (*see* page 9). Pipe royal icing name of choice on roof top.

Before commencing any work on this page, please read the whole sequence of instructions and ensure the proper materials and equipment are to hand, as well as sufficient time to complete the cake. Additional information can be found on pages 4-11 (Index on page 120).

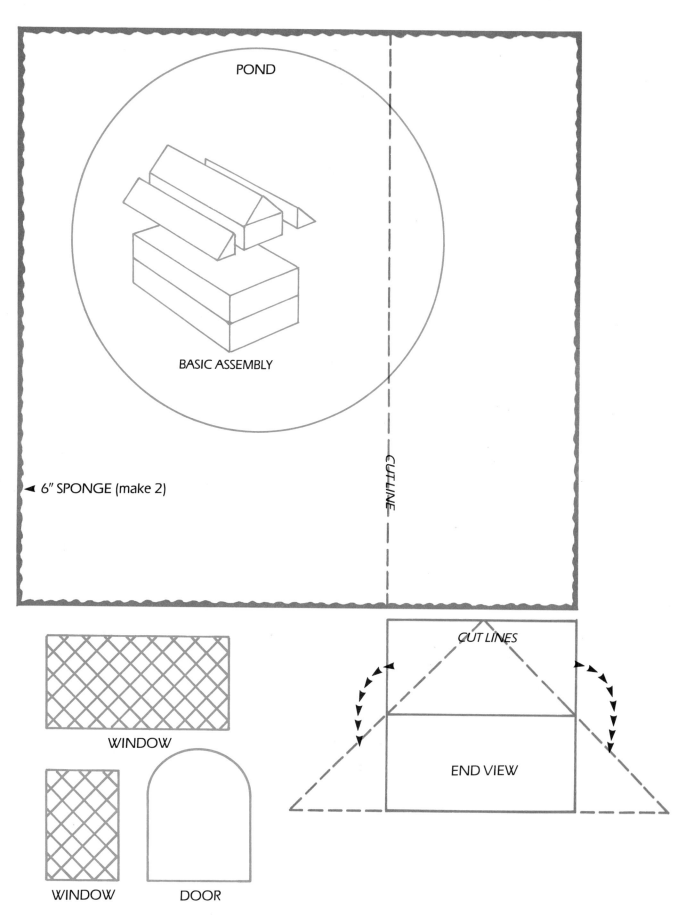

POND

BASIC ASSEMBLY

CUT LINE

◄ 6" SPONGE (make 2)

WINDOW

WINDOW

DOOR

CUT LINES

END VIEW

MACHO

Cake Requirements

7″ square sponge
14″ round board
16″ round doyley
Buttercream

Edible colours
Black – Blue – Brown – Caramel – Pink – Red

Royal icing
Sugar paste

1. Cut sponge to the shape shown and move off-cut to top to form the head.

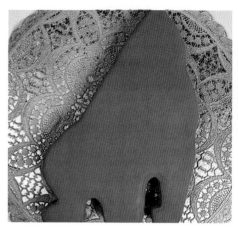

2. Trim to the template shape, then slice, fill and cover sponge with buttercream. Cover with sugar paste and place on doyley and board.

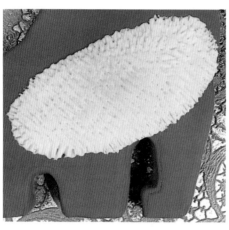

3. Roll out, cut and fix sugar paste tummy fur and mark with a cocktail stick.

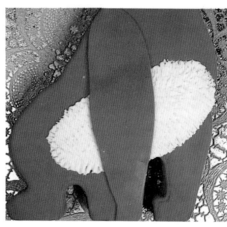

4. Roll out, cut and fix sugar paste arm.

5. Roll out, cut and fix sugar paste face and then pipe royal icing eyes and face lines.

6. Mould and fix sugar paste fingers and toes.

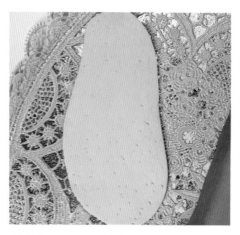

7. Roll out, cut and place a sugar paste 'nut' on to the doyley and prick with a fork.

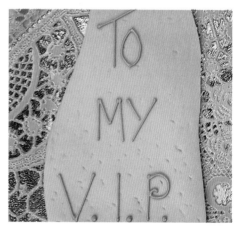

8. Pipe inscription of choice on nut with royal icing.

Before commencing any work on this page, please read the whole sequence of instructions and ensure the proper materials and equipment are to hand, as well as sufficient time to complete the cake. Additional information can be found on pages 4-11 (Index on page 120).

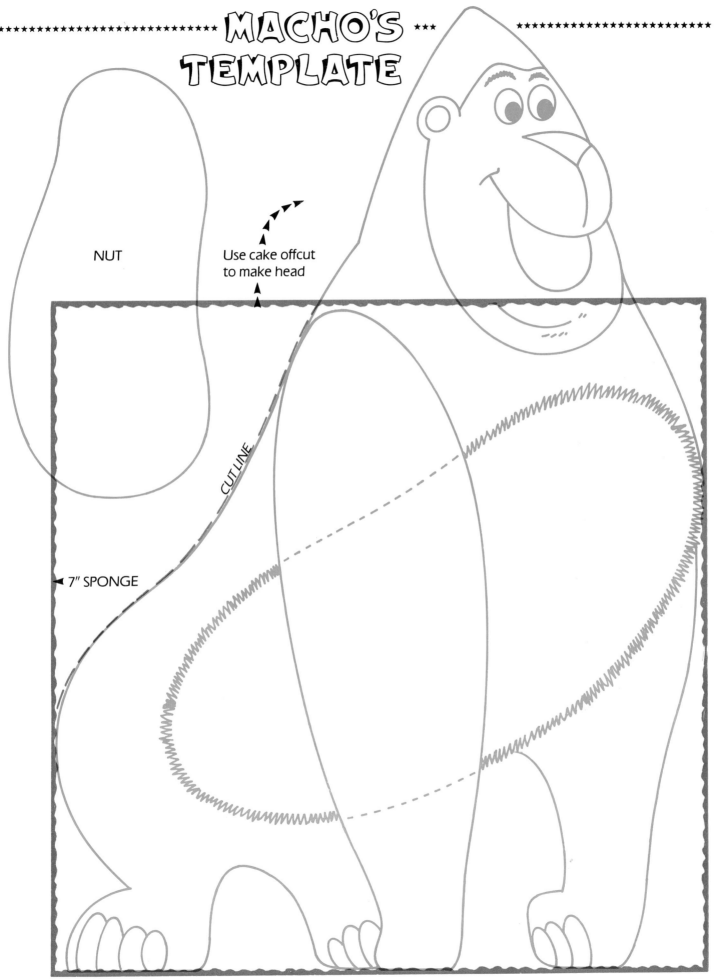

MACHO'S TEMPLATE

NUT

Use cake offcut to make head

CUT LINE

◄ 7" SPONGE

MELINDA

Cake Requirements

8″ square sponge
12″ round board
Buttercream

Edible colours
Black – Blue – Green – Red – Yellow

Royal icing
Sugar paste

1. Cut sponge to the shape shown, then slice, fill and cover with buttercream.

2. Position pieces as shown. Cover with sugar paste and place on board.

3. Roll out, cut and fix sugar paste organ sides.

4. Roll out, cut and fix sugar paste white key board, then mark keys with the back of a knife.

5. Roll out, cut and fix separate black sugar paste keys in the positions shown.

6. Roll out, cut and fix sugar paste control panel buttons.

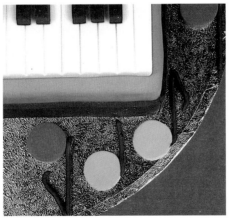

7. Roll out, cut and fix sugar paste discs to cake board and then pipe royal icing lines to form musical notes.

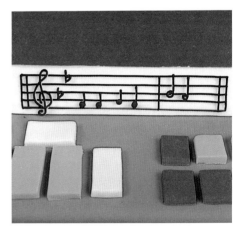

8. Roll out and cut a sugar paste "music sheet" and then pipe royal icing music. Leave to dry and then fix in position shown.

Before commencing any work on this page, please read the whole sequence of instructions and ensure the proper materials and equipment are to hand, as well as sufficient time to complete the cake. Additional information can be found on pages 4-11 (Index on page 120).

BASIC ASSEMBLY

SIDE

MUSIC SHEET

FRONT

KEYBOARD

◄ 8" SPONGE

‑ ‑ ‑ ‑ ‑ ‑ ‑ ‑ ‑ CUT LINE ‑ ‑ ‑ ‑ ‑ ‑ ‑ ‑ ‑

NOTE

◄ CONTROL PANEL ►
BUTTONS

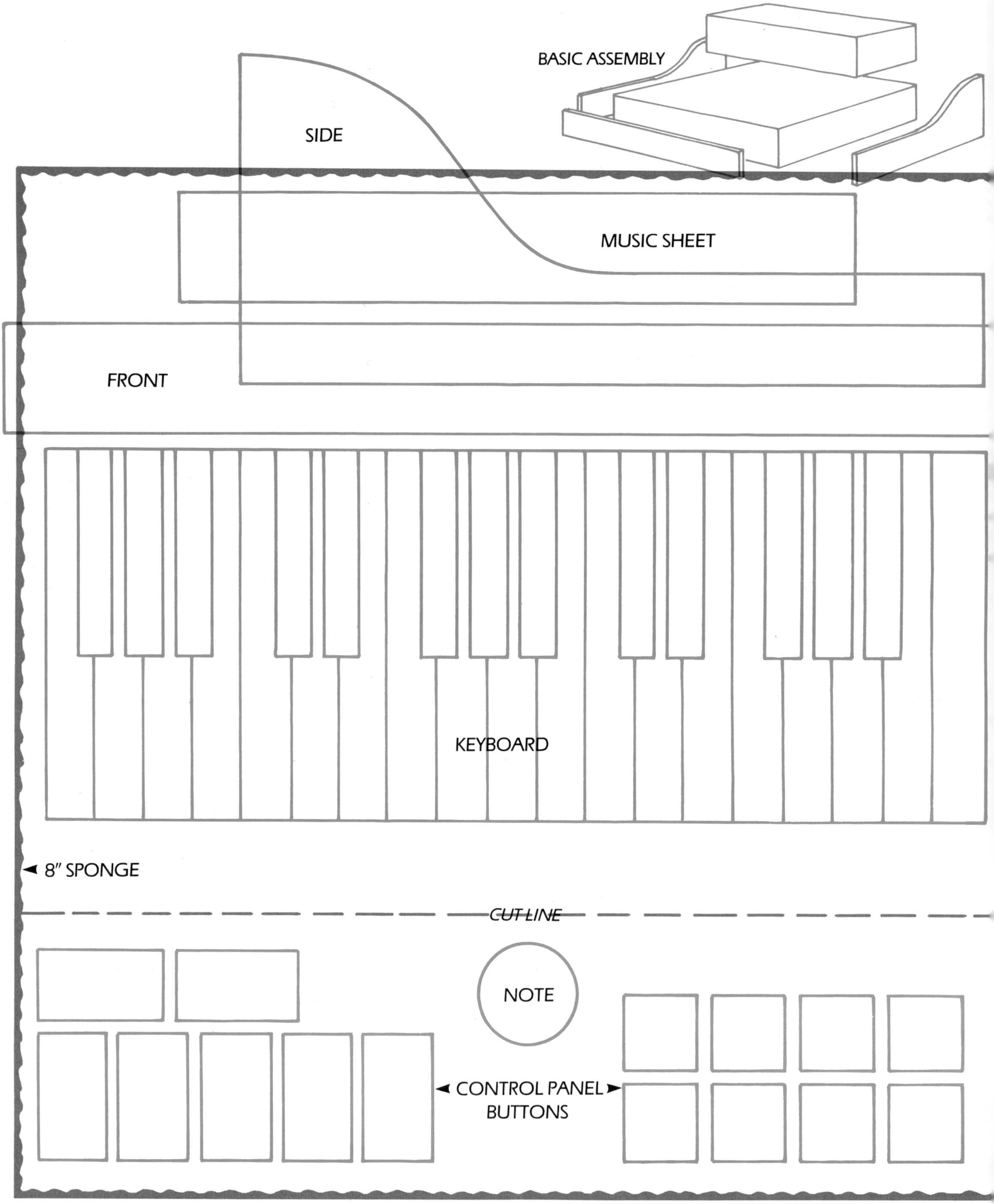

JOE

JOE

Cake Requirements

7″ square sponge
12″ × 14″ board
One metre of 1″ satin ribbon
Buttercream

Edible colours
Blue – Brown – Cream – Red

Royal icing
Sugar paste

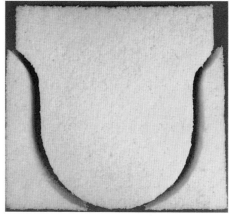

1. Cut sponge to the shape shown. Cut tips off the off-cuts and join to the cup's rim.

2. Position remaining off-cuts to form the stem. Slice, fill and coat sponge with buttercream. Place sponge on board.

3. Cover cup with two colours of sugar paste.

4. Roll out and fix sugar paste handles and bands, as shown.

5. Roll out, cut and fix a sugar paste figure "1" and pipe "ST" with royal icing.

6. Cut and fix satin ribbon to cup.

7. Pipe inscription of choice in royal icing at the base of the cup.

8. Decorate a piece of white card with piped royal icing, as shown and then add artificial decorations of choice.

Before commencing any work on this page, please read the whole sequence of instructions and ensure the proper materials and equipment are to hand, as well as sufficient time to complete the cake. Additional information can be found on pages 4-11 (Index on page 120).

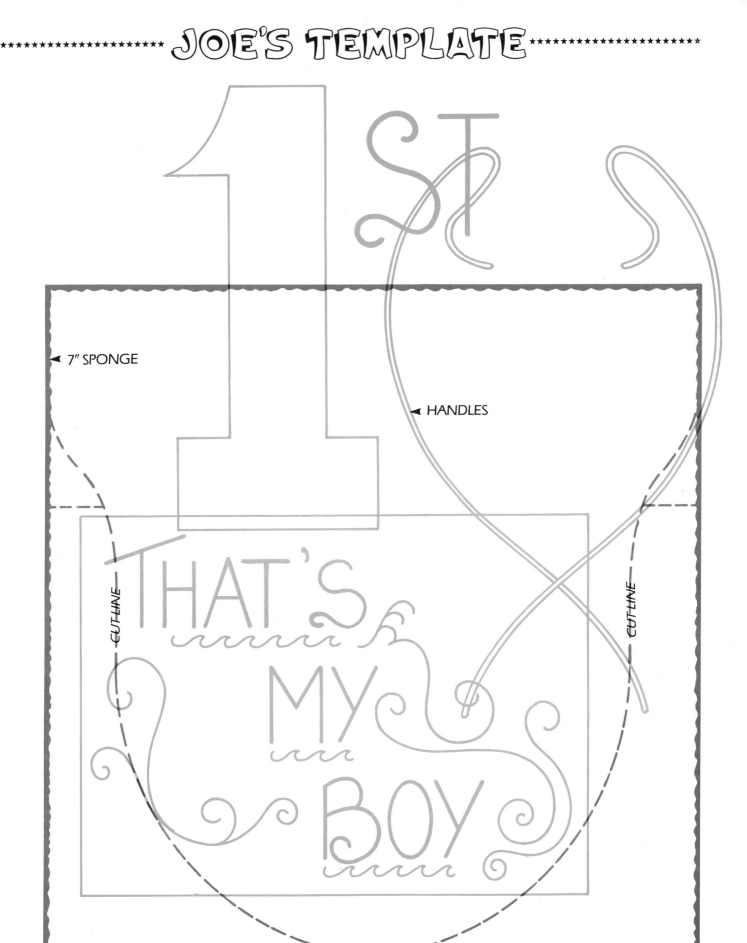

7" SPONGE

HANDLES

CUT-LINE

THAT'S MY BOY

CUT-LINE

TRICIA

TRICIA

Cake Requirements

7″ heart-shaped sponge
11″ round board
11″ round doyley
One metre ½″ satin ribbon
Buttercream

Edible colours
Black – French pink – Green – Lilac
Royal icing
Sugar paste

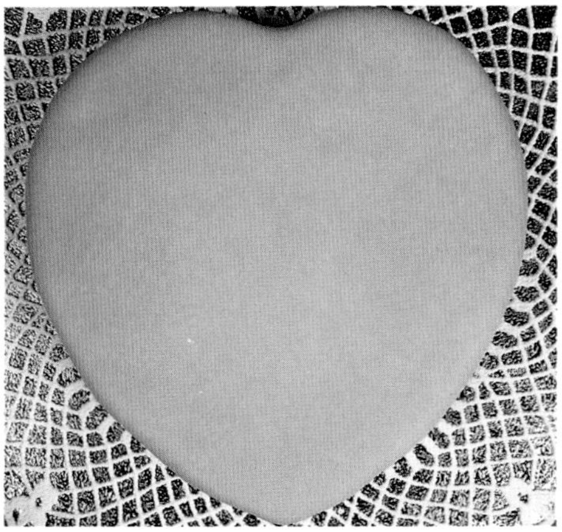

1. Slice, fill and cover sponge with buttercream, then cover with sugar paste and place on doyley and board.

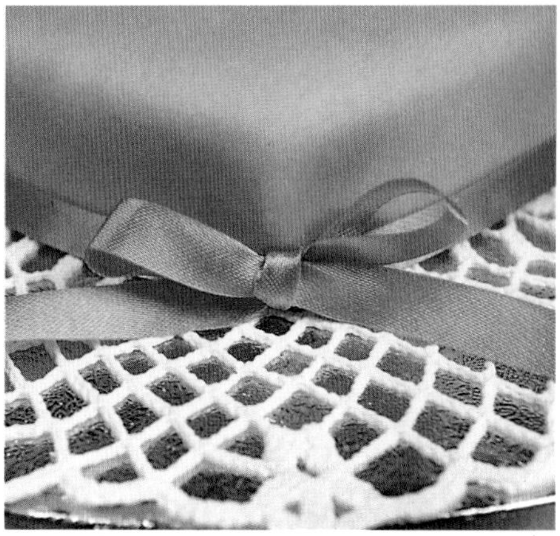

2. Carefully and gently fix satin ribbon around sponge base and tie in a bow, as shown.

3. Roll out, cut and fix a sugar paste card in the position shown.

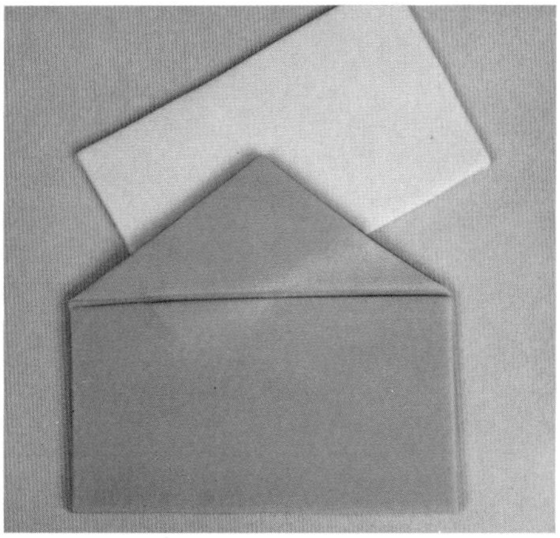

4. Roll out, cut, mark and fix a sugar paste envelope.

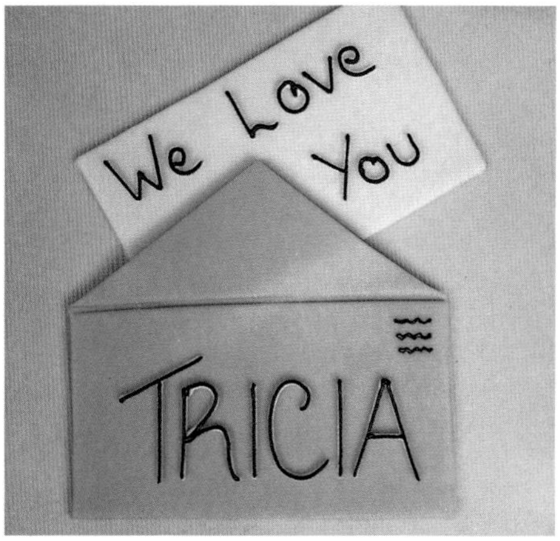

5. Pipe royal icing inscription and name of choice.

6. Pipe royal icing curved lines, as shown.

7. Pipe royal icing dots to form flower heads.

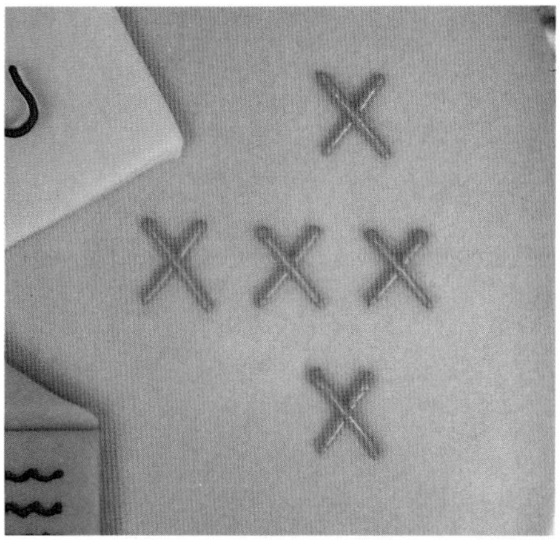

8. Pipe royal icing kisses to complete cake.

Before commencing any work on this page, please read the whole sequence of instructions and ensure the proper materials and equipment are to hand, as well as sufficient time to complete the cake. Additional information can be found on pages 4-11 (Index on page 120).

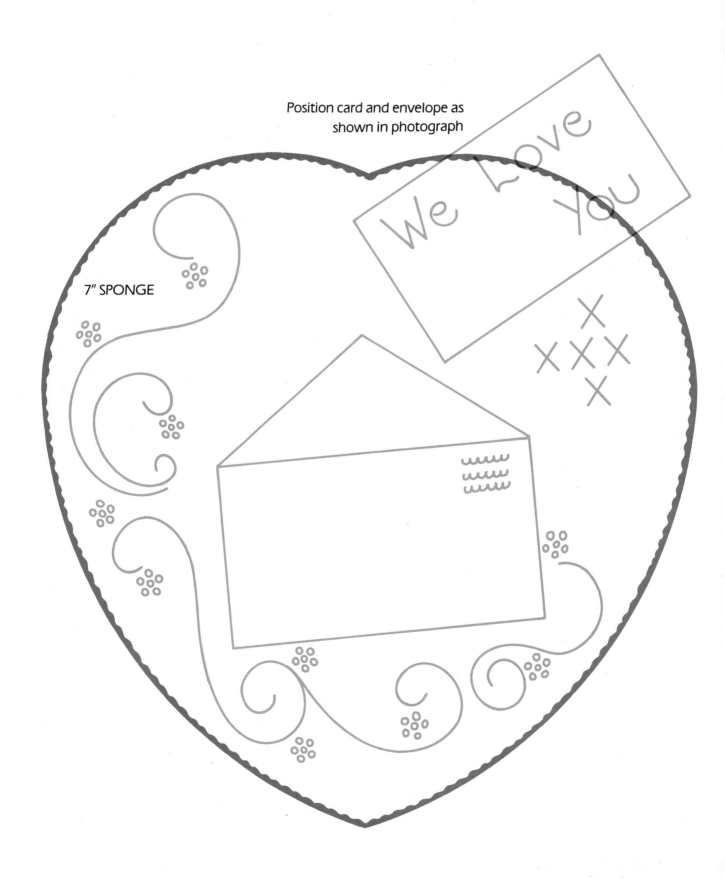

Position card and envelope as
shown in photograph

7" SPONGE

We Love You

BERNARD

Cake Requirements

8″ round sponge
12″ round board
12″ round doyley
Buttercream

Edible colours
Black – Brown – Christmas red – Cream

Royal icing
Sugar paste

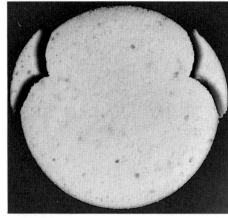

1. Cut sponge to the shape shown.

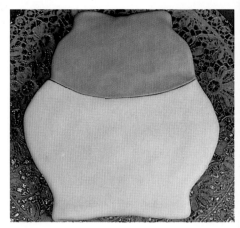

2. Cut each off-cut in half and use to form ears and feet. Slice and fill owl and then cover with sugar paste.

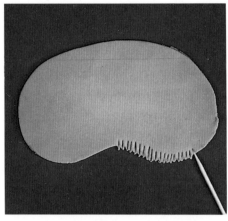

3. Place owl on doyley and cake-board. Cut out sugar paste face and mark edge with a cocktail stick.

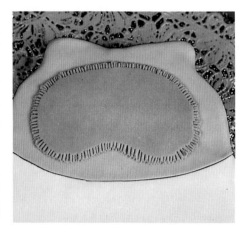

4. Fix face to owl.

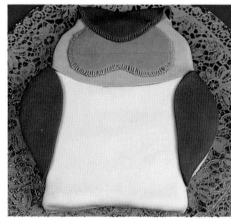

5. Cut out sugar paste 'cap', mark edge with a cocktail stick, then fold and fix as shown. Cut and fix sugar paste wings.

6. Repeat process in 2nd sentence of No. 3 to form beard and fix in position shown. Cut out and fix sugar paste eyes and beak.

7. Pipe inscription of choice, then wing and breast feathers with royal icing.

8. Make and fix a sugar paste branch and add sugar paste feet. Pipe royal icing claws.

Before commencing any work on this page, please read the whole sequence of instructions and ensure the proper materials and equipment are to hand, as well as sufficient time to complete the cake. Additional information can be found on pages 4-11 (Index on page 120).

CUT LINES

CUT LINES

◄ 8" SPONGE

ELLEN

Cake Requirements

8″ square sponge
15″ round board
16″ round doyley
Buttercream

Edible colours
Black – Blue – Brown – Pink – Red – Violet – Yellow

Royal icing
Sugar paste

1. Cut sponge in half. Sandwich, fill and cover with buttercream.

2. Cover sponge with sugar paste. Place on doyley and board.

3. Roll out, cut and fix sugar paste lid and straps.

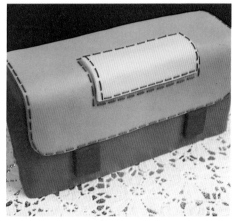

4. Roll out, cut and fix a sugar paste label. Pipe royal icing dashes around the satchel lid and label to form stitches.

5. Pipe name on satchel label with royal icing and then decorate, as shown.

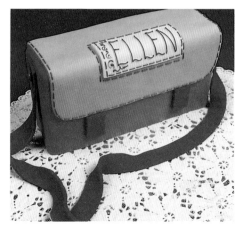

6. Roll out, cut and fix a sugar paste shoulder strap in position shown.

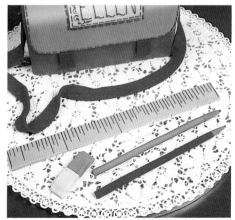

7. Make various pieces of sugar paste school equipment and place on the doyley.

8. Make and place a sugar paste book against the satchel and decorate the book with piped royal icing.

Before commencing any work on this page, please read the whole sequence of instructions and ensure the proper materials and equipment are to hand, as well as sufficient time to complete the cake. Additional information can be found on pages 4-11 (Index on page 120).

ELLEN'S TEMPLATE

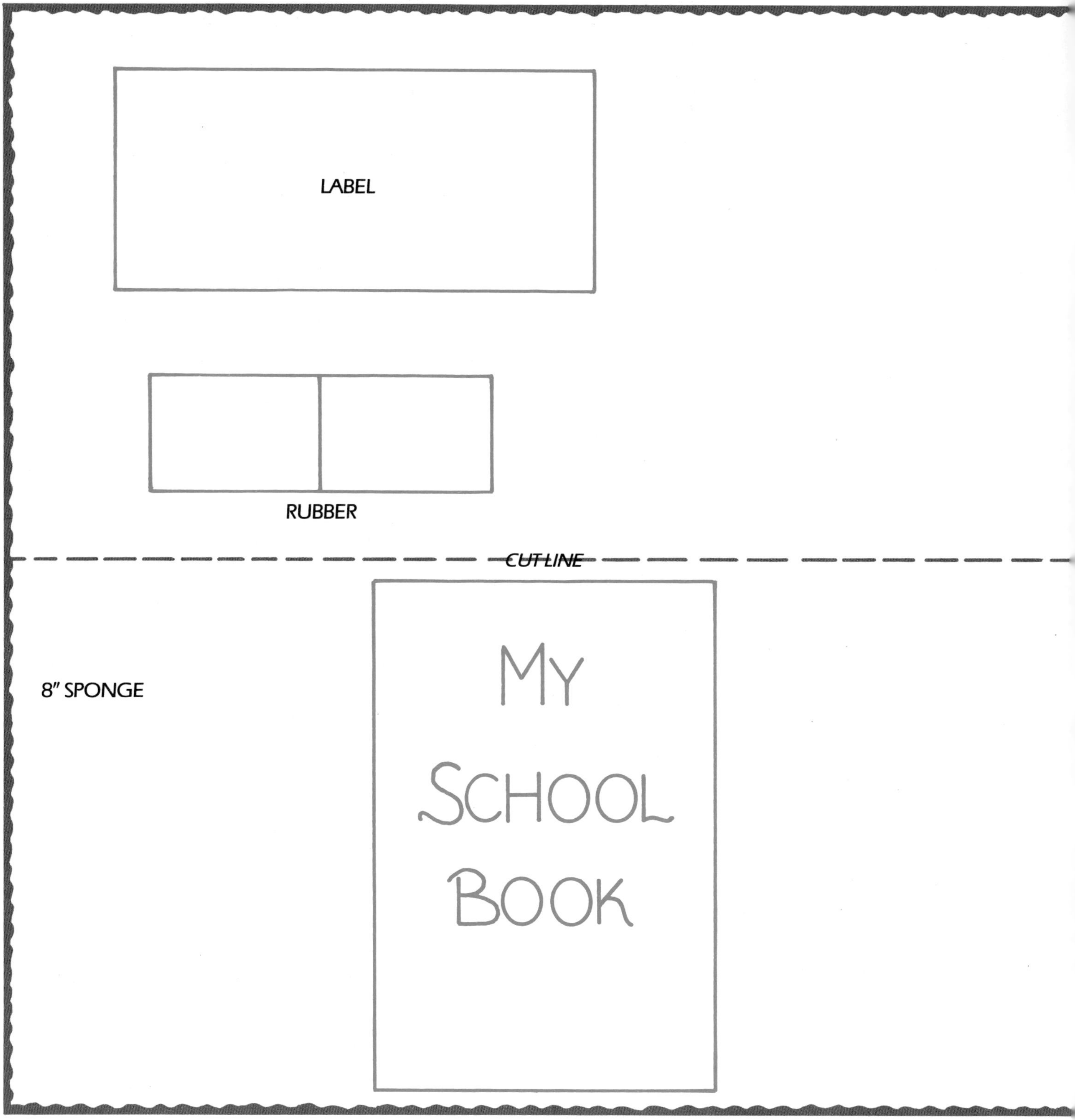
LABEL
RUBBER
CUT LINE
8" SPONGE
MY
SCHOOL
BOOK

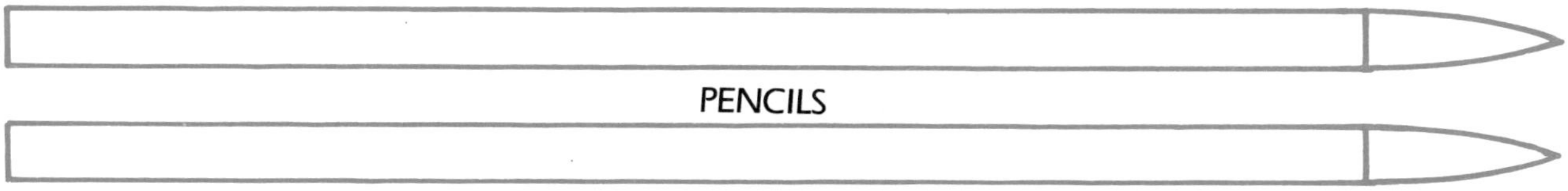
PENCILS

JIMMY

Cake Requirements

Two × 6″ square sponges
14″ square board
Buttercream
Cake candles and holders

Edible colours
*Black – Blue – Brown – Christmas red
– Green – Moss green – Orange – Yellow*

Royal icing
Sugar paste

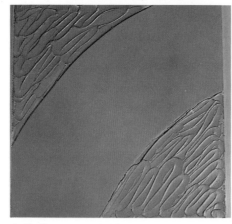

1. Roll out, cut and fix sugar paste race track. Spread royal icing on remaining areas with a palette knife.

2. Cut each sponge to the shapes shown, then slice and fill. Position pieces to form the car and cover with buttercream.

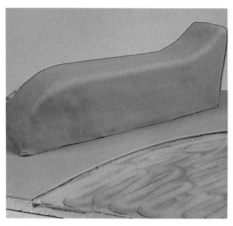

3. Cover car with sugar paste and place on track.

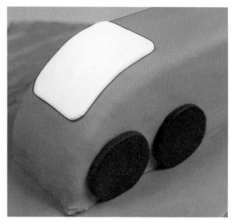

4. Roll out, cut and fix sugar paste driver's hatch, wheels and wheel hubs.

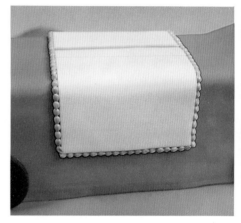

5. Roll out, cut and fix sugar paste engine cowl. Pipe royal icing edge shells and a centre line.

6. Mould and fix driver's sugar paste head, helmet and scarf. Pipe in face features with royal icing.

7. Pipe recipient's name and age in royal icing. Pipe small shells around edge of car's rear.

8. Make sugar paste bushes (see page 9) and fix. Roll out, cut and fix sugar paste curb stones. Fix candle holders and candles, as shown.

WARNING – CANDLES WILL BURN RAPIDLY CAUSING WAX TO DRIP

Before commencing any work on this page, please read the whole sequence of instructions and ensure the proper materials and equipment are to hand, as well as sufficient time to complete the cake. Additional information can be found on pages 4-11 (Index on page 120).

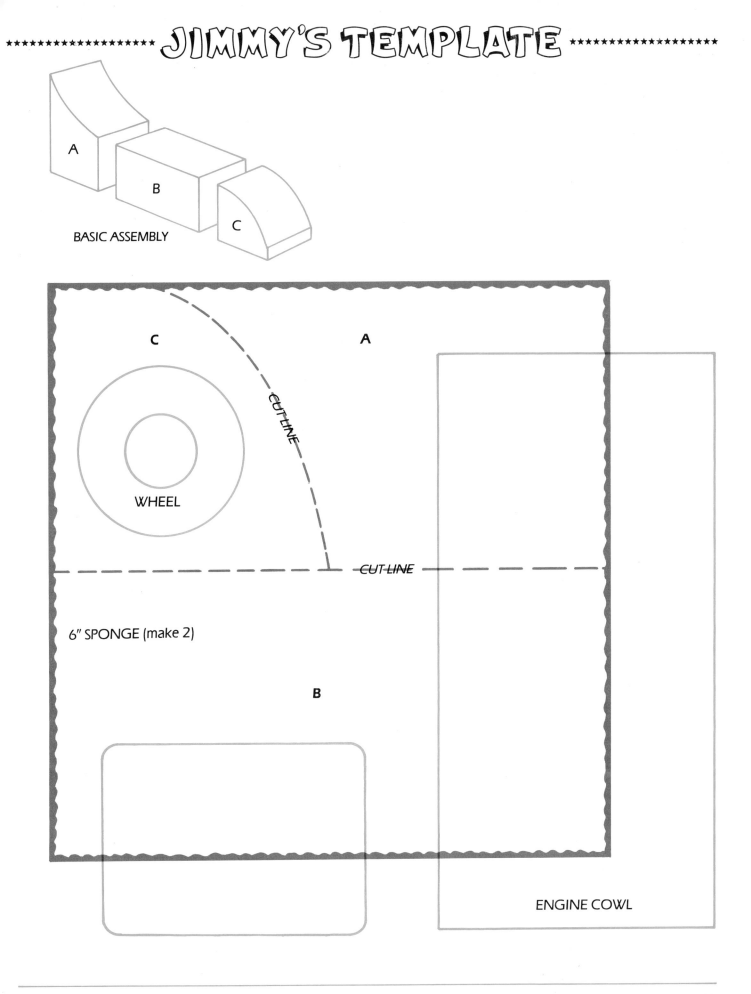

BASIC ASSEMBLY

A

B

C

C

WHEEL

A

CUT LINE

CUT LINE

6" SPONGE (make 2)

B

ENGINE COWL

TRUDY

Cake Requirements

Sponge baked in 2pt pudding basin.
11″ round board
12″ round doyley
9″ round doyley
Buttercream
Doll bust

Edible colours
French pink – Green – Lilac – Yellow

Royal icing
Sugar paste

1. Slice, fill and coat sponge with buttercream and then cover with sugar paste. Place on both doyleys and board.

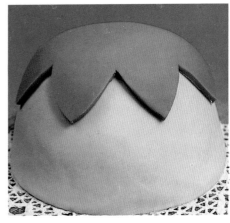

2. Roll out, cut and fix sugar paste dress top.

3. Using a petal tube, pipe royal icing edging to dress. Fix china or plastic figure to cake cake-top.

4. Using a petal tube, pipe two rows of royal icing edging around cake-base.

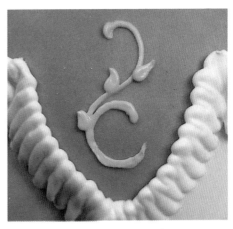

5. Pipe royal icing stems and leaves in each skirt section.

6. Pipe royal icing flowers and bows in each section, as shown.

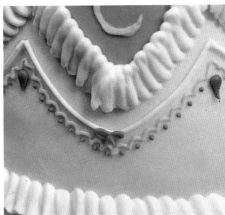

7. Pipe royal icing lines, dots and bows around skirt edging.

8. Roll out, cut and fix sufficient sugar paste discs to spell required name and then pipe an initial on each disc with royal icing.

Before commencing any work on this page, please read the whole sequence of instructions and ensure the proper materials and equipment are to hand, as well as sufficient time to complete the cake. Additional information can be found on pages 4-11 (Index on page 120).

BENNY

Cake Requirements

8″ round sponge
12″ round board
12″ round doyley
Buttercream

Edible colours
Black – Blue – Brown – Flesh – Green – Orange – Red – Yellow

Royal icing
Sugar paste

1. Cut sponge to the shape shown. Slice, fill and coat each piece with buttercream.

2. Cover each piece with sugar paste and place on to doyley and board in position shown.

3. Cut and fix the sugar paste clock face and then pipe numbers with royal icing.

4. Roll out, cut and fix sugar paste eyes and mouth and then pipe eye centres and nose with royal icing.

5. Roll out, cut and fix sugar paste arms, hands, legs and feet.

6. Mould and fix the sugar paste hammer and pipe clock hands with royal icing.

7. Pipe "WAKEY WAKEY" on alarm.

8. Roll out, cut and place a sugar paste plaque on the doyley, then pipe inscription of choice with royal icing where shown.

Before commencing any work on this page, please read the whole sequence of instructions and ensure the proper materials and equipment are to hand, as well as sufficient time to complete the cake. Additional information can be found on pages 4-11 (Index on page 120).

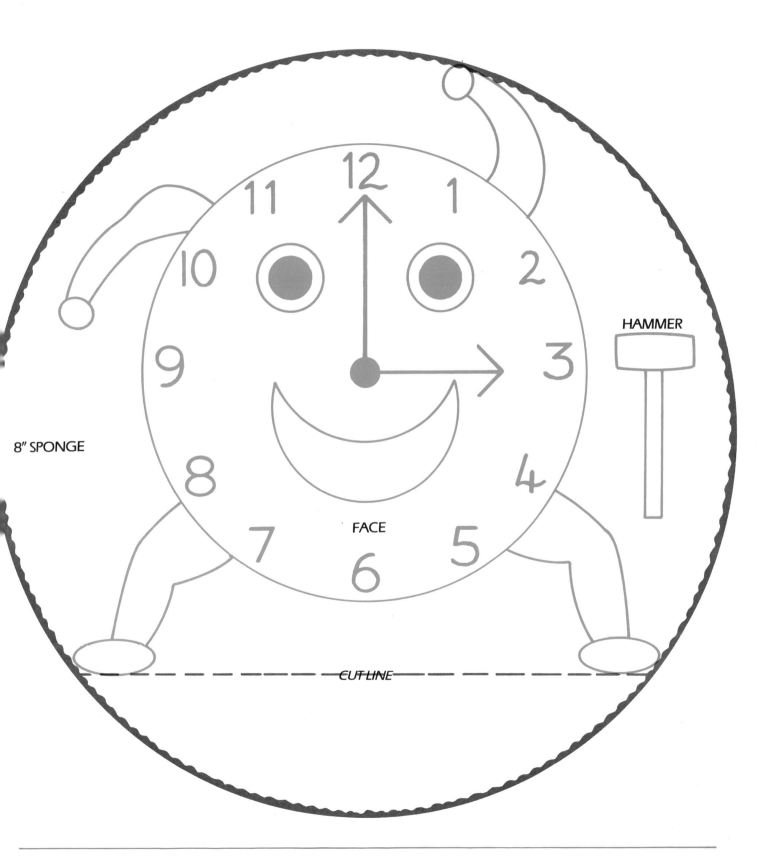

8" SPONGE

HAMMER

FACE

CUT LINE

PRISCILLA

Cake Requirements

8″ square sponge
14″ round board
14″ round doyley
One metre of 1″ satin ribbon
Buttercream
Confectioner's dusting powder

Edible colours
French pink – Green – Lilac – Yellow

Royal icing
Sugar paste

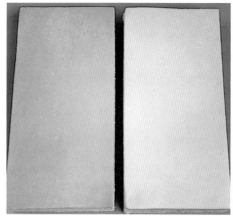

1. Cut sponge in half and cover the top of each half with buttercream. Then cover the top of each half with a different coloured sugar paste.

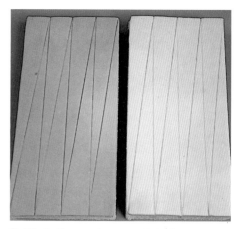

2. Mark, then cut sponge into the triangular wedges shown.

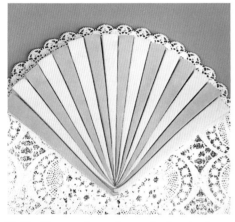

3. Position each wedge on to the doyley and cake-board to form a fan, as shown.

4. Roll out, cut and fix sugar paste along each fan side and at the 'hinge'.

5. Pipe royal icing shells along each fan section.

6. Cut and fix sugar paste flower centres. Pipe royal icing lines and dots to form flowers and then brush dusting powder on to each petal.

7. Pipe royal icing stems and leaves across the fan top, as shown.

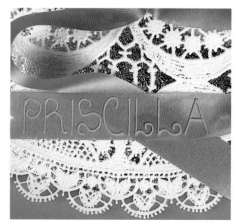

8. Shape and fix the ribbon in the position shown. Then pipe royal icing name of choice on to ribbon, as shown.

Before commencing any work on this page, please read the whole sequence of instructions and ensure the proper materials and equipment are to hand, as well as sufficient time to complete the cake. Additional information can be found on pages 4-11 (Index on page 120).

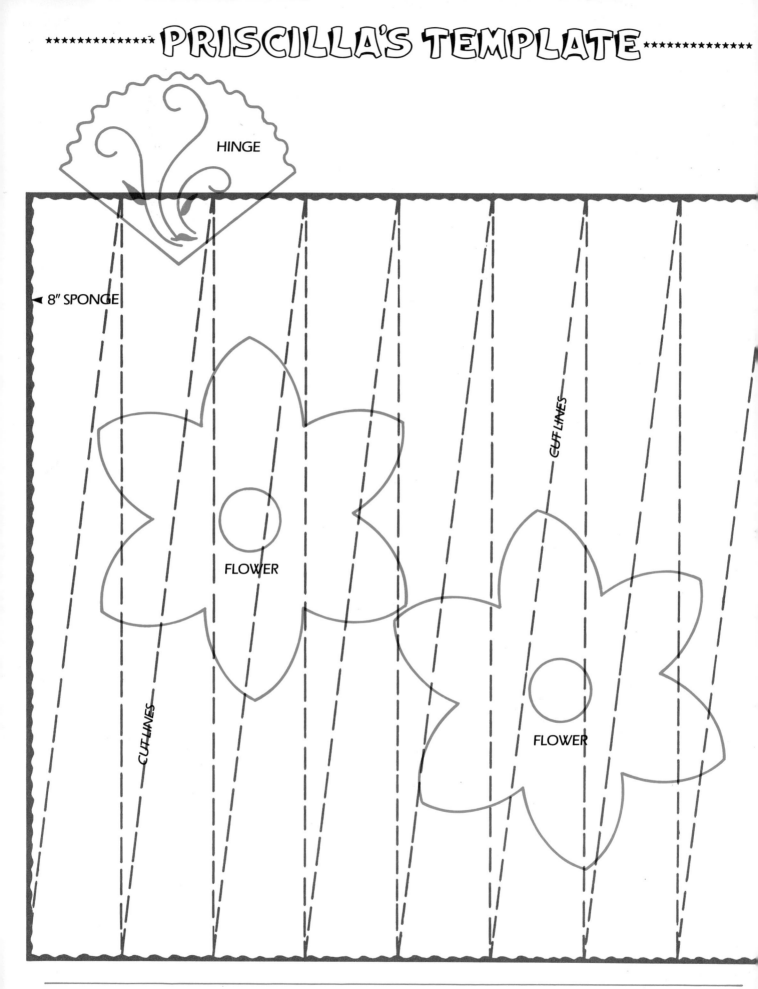

HINGE

◄ 8" SPONGE

FLOWER

FLOWER

CUT LINES

CUT LINES

TOBY

Cake Requirements

8″ × 5″ sponge
10″ square board
Buttercream

Edible colours
Black – Blue – Caramel – Green – Red – Yellow

Royal icing
Sugar paste

1. Cut end off sponge at the angle shown, reverse off-cut and place on top of sponge in position shown in figure No. 2.

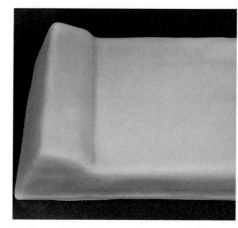

2. Slice, fill and coat sponge with buttercream. Cover in sugar paste and place on board.

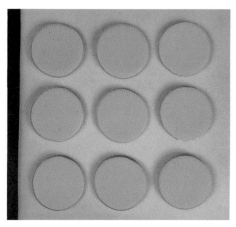

3. Roll out, cut and fix sugar paste discs, as shown.

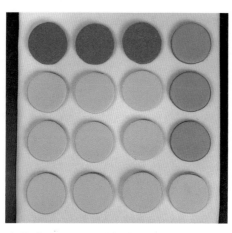

4. Roll out, cut and fix further sugar paste discs, as shown.

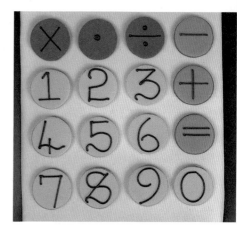

5. Pipe royal icing digits and mathematical signs, as shown.

6. Roll out, cut and fix the sugar paste calculator window.

7. Pipe royal icing digits and signs on window to equal the birthday age.

8. Roll out, cut and fix sugar paste "ON" and "OFF" buttons and plaque. Pipe "ON", "OFF" and inscription of choice with royal icing.

64   **Before commencing any work on this page, please read the whole sequence of instructions and ensure the proper materials and equipment are to hand, as well as sufficient time to complete the cake. Additional information can be found on pages 4-11 (Index on page 120).**

TOBY'S TEMPLATE

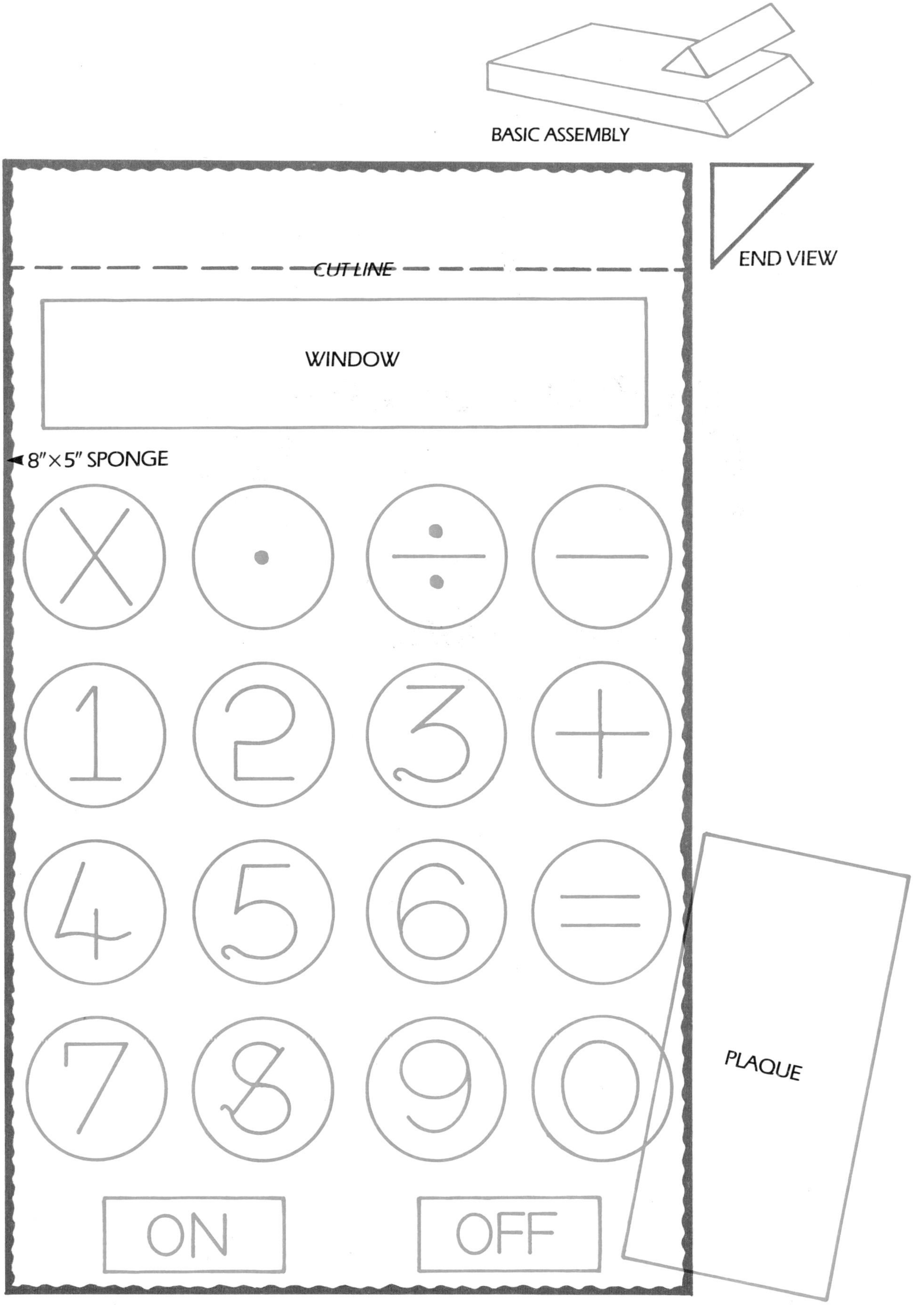

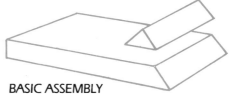

BASIC ASSEMBLY

END VIEW

CUT LINE

WINDOW

◄ 8″×5″ SPONGE

⊗ ⊙ ÷ ⊖

1 2 3 +

4 5 6 =

7 8 9 0

ON   OFF

PLAQUE

Cake Requirements

4″ round sponge
5″ round sponge
4″ square sponge
12″ × 14″ board
Buttercream

Edible colours
Black – Brown – Cream – Red – Yellow

Royal icing
Sugar paste

1. Cut the 5″ round sponge to hold the 4″ round sponge (thus forming an '8' outline). Cut the square sponge in half.

2. Slice, fill and coat the '8' with buttercream, then cover with sugar paste to form the guitar sound box. Position on board.

3. Slice, fill, join (end to end) and coat the square sponge with buttercream. Place on board and cover with sugar paste, as shown.

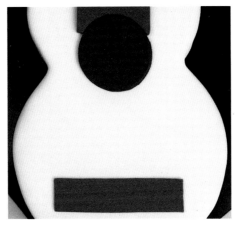

4. Roll out, cut and fix sugar paste pieces, as shown.

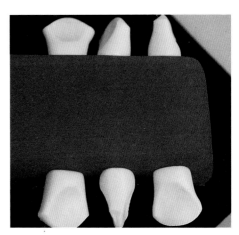

5. Roll out, cut, form and fix sugar paste string keys.

6. Pipe the royal icing lines shown.

7. Pipe the royal icing strings and dots shown.

8. Roll out, cut and place sugar paste cards on board. Decorate each card with royal icing inscriptions and musical notes.

Before commencing any work on this page, please read the whole sequence of instructions and ensure the proper materials and equipment are to hand, as well as sufficient time to complete the cake. Additional information can be found on pages 4-11 (Index on page 120).

67

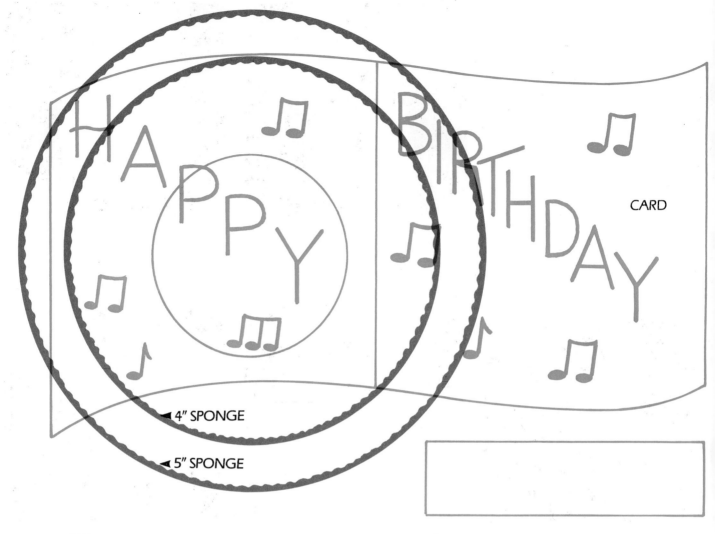

CARD

◄ 4" SPONGE

◄ 5" SPONGE

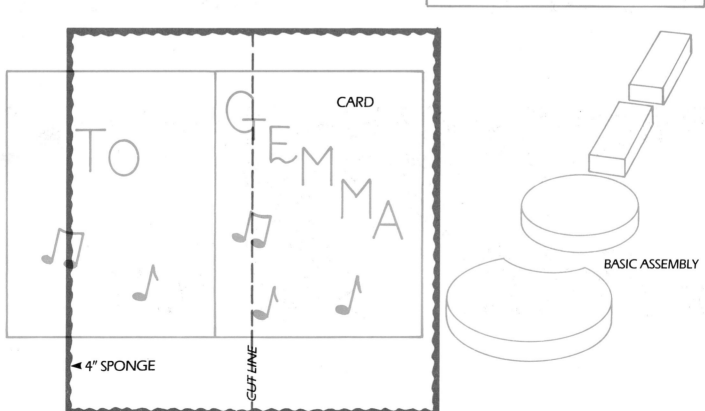

CARD

TO GEMMA

◄ 4" SPONGE

CUT LINE

BASIC ASSEMBLY

NOAH

Cake Requirements

8″ square sponge
14″ round board
2 candle holders & candles
Buttercream

Edible colours
Black – Blue – Brown – Cream – French
Pink – Green – Red – Yellow

Royal icing
Sugar paste

1. Cut sponge to the shape shown.

2. Position pieces to form hull and boat house. Slice, fill and cover with buttercream.

3. Roll out, cut and fix sugar paste to the hull and boat house. Then join sponges together to form the Ark.

4. Place ark on the board. Spread royal icing over the remainder of the board with a palette knife, to form sea and land.

5. Roll out, cut and fix sugar paste doors and windows, then pipe royal icing decorations, as shown.

6. Pipe inscriptions of choice with royal icing on roof and bow.

7. Roll out, cut, mark and fix the sugar paste ramp to a pre-cut cake-card and place in position shown. Decorate land with royal icing.

8. Add moulded sugar paste animals and Noah (see p.71 for instructions). Fix candle holders and candles.

Before commencing any work on this page, please read the whole sequence of instructions and ensure the proper materials and equipment are to hand, as well as sufficient time to complete the cake. Additional information can be found on pages 4-11 (Index on page 120).

1. NOAH. Mould two balls of sugar paste to form body and head. Mould sugar paste to form arms. Fix together. Then mould and fix hands, feet and nose. Pipe royal icing hair, beard, moustache and eyes.

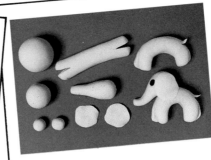

5. ELEPHANT. From large ball of sugar paste, mould body and cut legs. Cut tail. From medium ball, mould head and trunk and fix to body. Flatten small balls to form ears and fix. Pipe royal icing eyes.

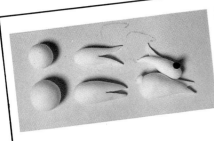

2. RABBIT. Form head from smaller ball of sugar paste and body from the larger ball. Cut each shape to form ears and legs. Fix. Mould and fix a tail and pipe royal icing eyes.

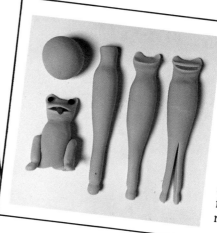

6. FROG. From a ball of sugar paste mould the pin shape shown. Squeeze top to form ears and mouth. Cut slit for mouth and another slit for the legs. Bend legs so that the frog is sitting. Mould and fix tongue and pipe royal icing eyes.

3. KANGAROO. From a ball of sugar paste, mould the shape shown. Cut the legs and ears, then bend to the position shown. Pipe royal icing eyes.

7. SEAL. From a ball of sugar paste, mould the shape shown. Cut tail and fins. Pipe royal icing eyes.

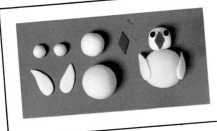

4. DUCK. Form wings, head and body from sugar paste. Fix together. Cut and fix a sugar paste beak. Pipe royal icing eyes.

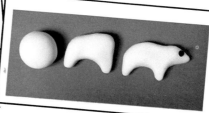

8. POLAR BEAR. From a ball of sugar paste, mould body, legs and head. Pipe royal icing eyes.

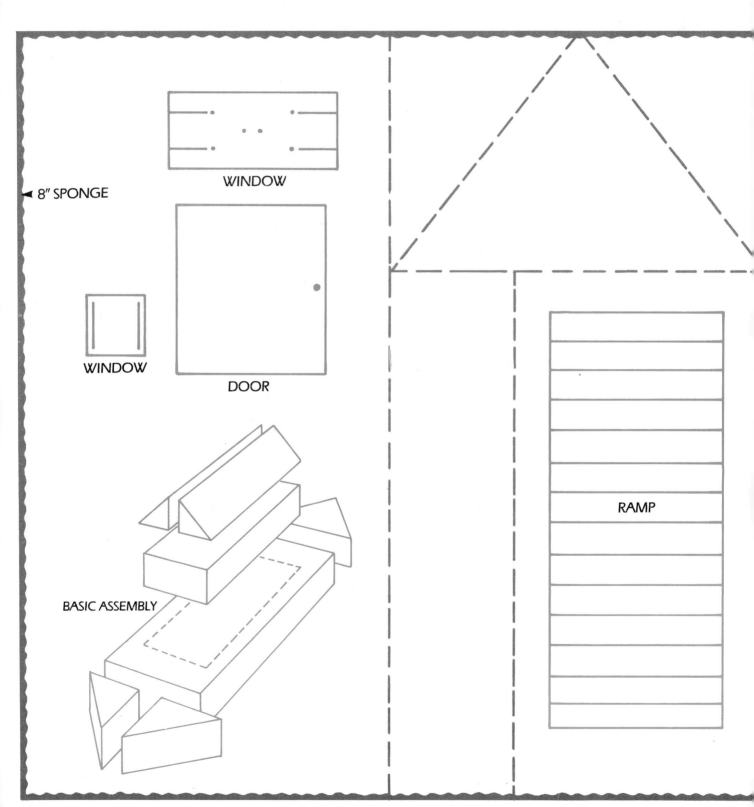

WINDOW

◄ 8" SPONGE

WINDOW

DOOR

BASIC ASSEMBLY

RAMP

MICHELLE

Cake Requirements

Three 6" square sponges
12" round board
12" round doyley
4 candle holders & candles
Buttercream

Edible colours
*Black – Brown – Caramel – French pink
– Green – Yellow*

Royal icing
Sugar paste

Photograph of the birthday child fixed
to a piece of tin foil.

1. Cut two sponges where shown and then place the off-cuts at each side of the third uncut sponge to form the T.V. base.

2. Slice fill and cover the T.V. base with buttercream and then cover with sugar paste. Place on doyley and board.

3. Sandwich the two cut sponges together with buttercream and place in an upright position to form the T.V. Cover in buttercream and sugar paste.

4. Place. T.V. on base. Fix photograph to the T.V. screen. Pipe royal icing shells around screen and T.V. edges.

5. Roll out, cut and fix a sugar paste control panel. Decorate panel with piped royal icing, as shown.

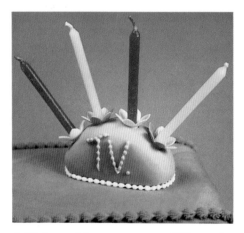

6. Make and fix a sugar paste T.V. aerial base. Fix candle holders and candles. Decorate with piped royal icing.

7. Pipe a royal icing inscription of choice with tracery decoration.

8. Roll out, cut and place a sugar paste newspaper on the doyley, then pipe a royal icing inscription of choice.

Before commencing any work on this page, please read the whole sequence of instructions and ensure the proper materials and equipment are to hand, as well as sufficient time to complete the cake. Additional information can be found on pages 4-11 (Index on page 120).

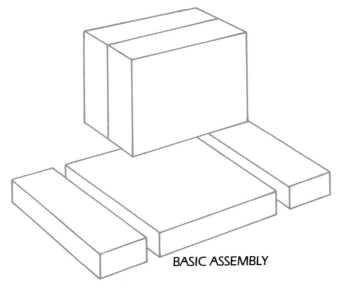

BASIC ASSEMBLY

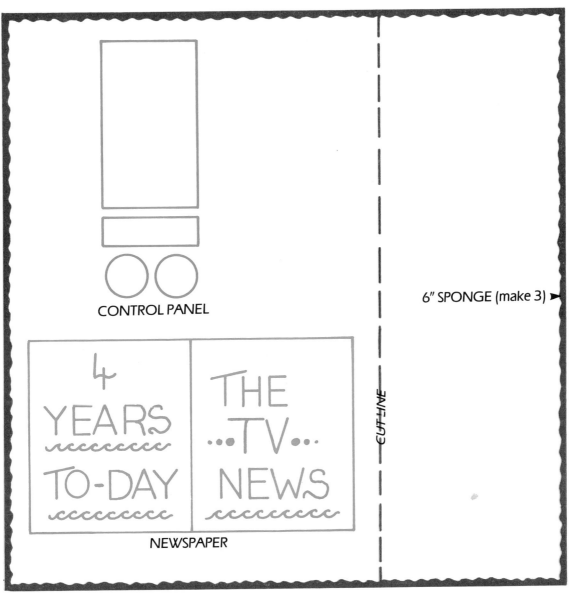

CONTROL PANEL

6" SPONGE (make 3) ►

4
YEARS
ᴄᴄᴄᴄᴄᴄᴄᴄ
TO-DAY
ᴄᴄᴄᴄᴄᴄᴄᴄ

THE
...TV...
NEWS
ᴄᴄᴄᴄᴄᴄᴄᴄ

NEWSPAPER

CUT-LINE

CHARLIE

Cake Requirements

6″ round sponge
6″ square sponge
15″ round board
15″ round doyley
Buttercream
Chocolate vermicelli

Edible colours
*Black – Blue – Brown – Cream – Flesh
– Green – Orange – Red – Violet*

Royal icing
Sugar paste

1. Cut each sponge into the shapes shown.

2. Re-position shapes to form the clown's hat, face and tie. (The square pieces are dealt with in No.7).

3. Slice, fill and cover each piece of the clown with buttercream, then cover each piece with sugar paste. Assemble clown on doyley and board.

4. Cut/mould and fix sugar paste eyebrows, eyes and nose.

5. Roll out, cut and fix sugar paste pieces to form the mouth and bow tie decoration. Pipe royal icing lines on mouth, as shown.

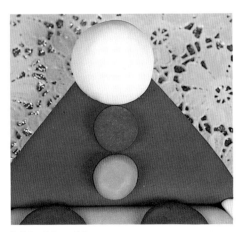

6. Mould and fix sugar paste pompoms to hat.

7. Cover each square with buttercream and then dip the sides of each square into vermicelli. Cover each top with sugar paste.

8. Pipe a royal icing letter on each square to form the name and number for the age. Place squares around clown.

Before commencing any work on this page, please read the whole sequence of instructions and ensure the proper materials and equipment are to hand, as well as sufficient time to complete the cake. Additional information can be found on pages 4-11 (Index on page 120).

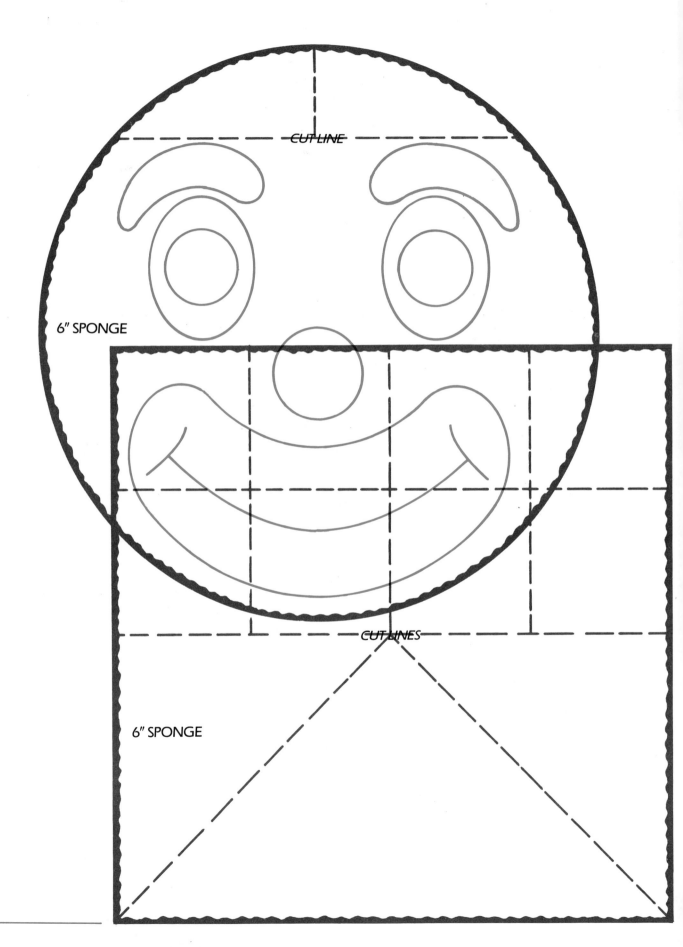

CUT LINE

6" SPONGE

CUT LINES

6" SPONGE

STACY

Cake Requirements

8″ square sponge
14″ round board
14″ round doyley
Buttercream

Edible colours
Black – Raspberry pink

Royal icing
Sugar paste

1. Cut sponge to the shapes shown.

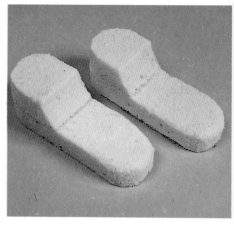

2. Place a small piece of sponge on to a large piece and trim to the shape shown. Repeat with the other two pieces of sponge.

3. Slice, fill and cover each shoe with buttercream and then cover with sugar paste. Place on doyley and board.

4. Roll out, cut and fix sugar paste pieces to form the heel and sole sides.

5. Roll out, form and fix sugar paste sports trainer uppers and toe caps.

6. Pipe royal icing dashes to represent stitching.

7. Pipe royal icing circles to form eye holes and an "S" (or appropriate initial) on each toe cap.

8. Pipe royal icing laces.

Before commencing any work on this page, please read the whole sequence of instructions and ensure the proper materials and equipment are to hand, as well as sufficient time to complete the cake. Additional information can be found on pages 4-11 (Index on page 120).

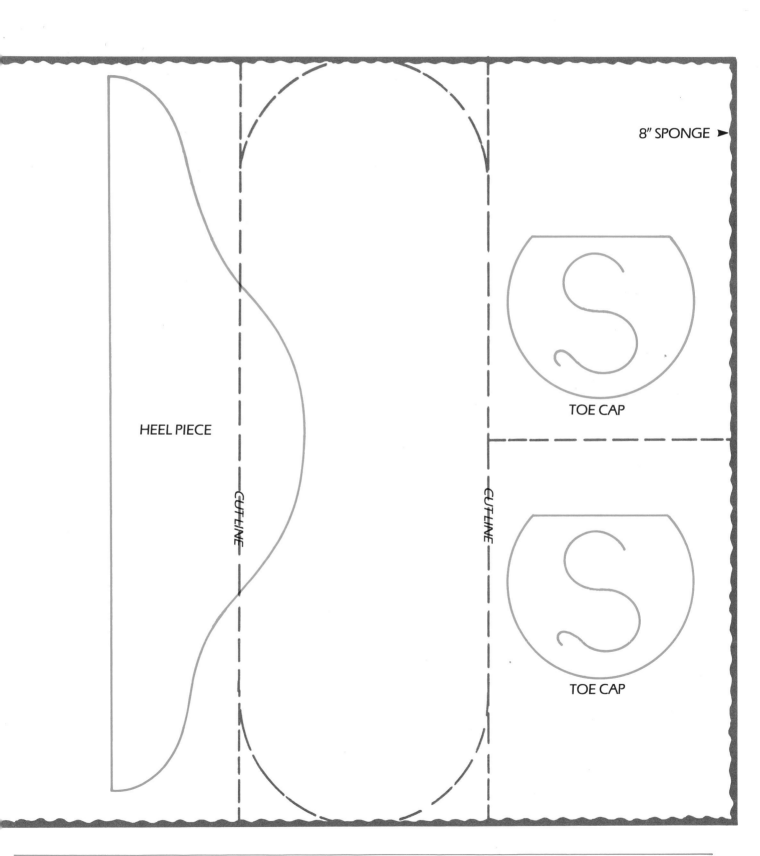

KEITH

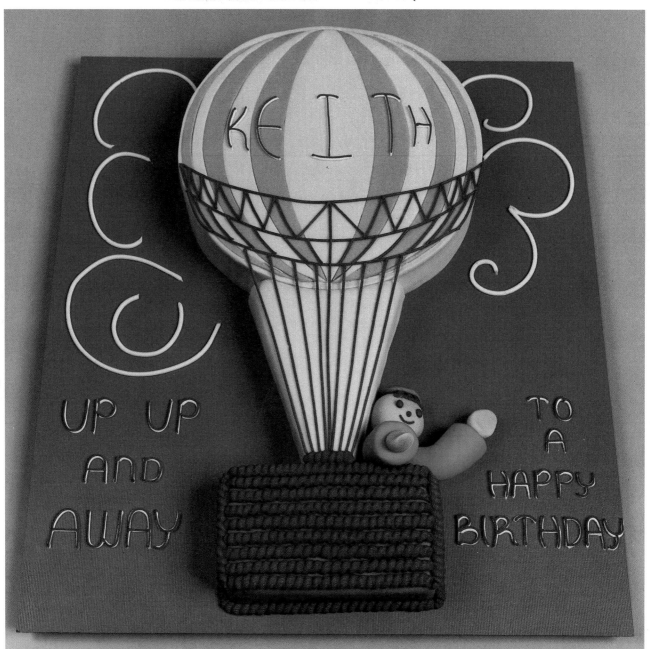

Cake Requirements

7″ round sponge
4″ square sponge
12″ × 14″ board
Buttercream

Edible colours
Blue – Brown – Green – Orange – Red – Yellow

Royal icing
Sugar paste

1. Cut square sponge to the shape shown. Position outer pieces to make the balloon basket. Slice, fill and coat sponges with buttercream.

2. Roll out, cut and fix sugar paste pieces in two colours to cover the balloon.

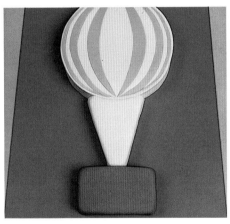

3. Roll out, cut and fix sugar paste to cover the central section and basket.

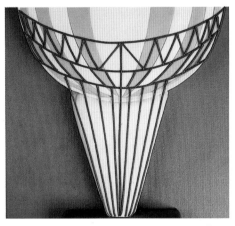

4. Pipe royal icing "support rope" lines, as shown.

5. Pipe royal icing rope lines over the basket.

6. Mould, fix and decorate with royal icing, a sugar paste person.

7. Pipe royal icing lines to form clouds.

8. Pipe name of choice on balloon in royal icing and then pipe inscription on board.

Before commencing any work on this page, please read the whole sequence of instructions and ensure the proper materials and equipment are to hand, as well as sufficient time to complete the cake. Additional information can be found on pages 4-11 (Index on page 120).

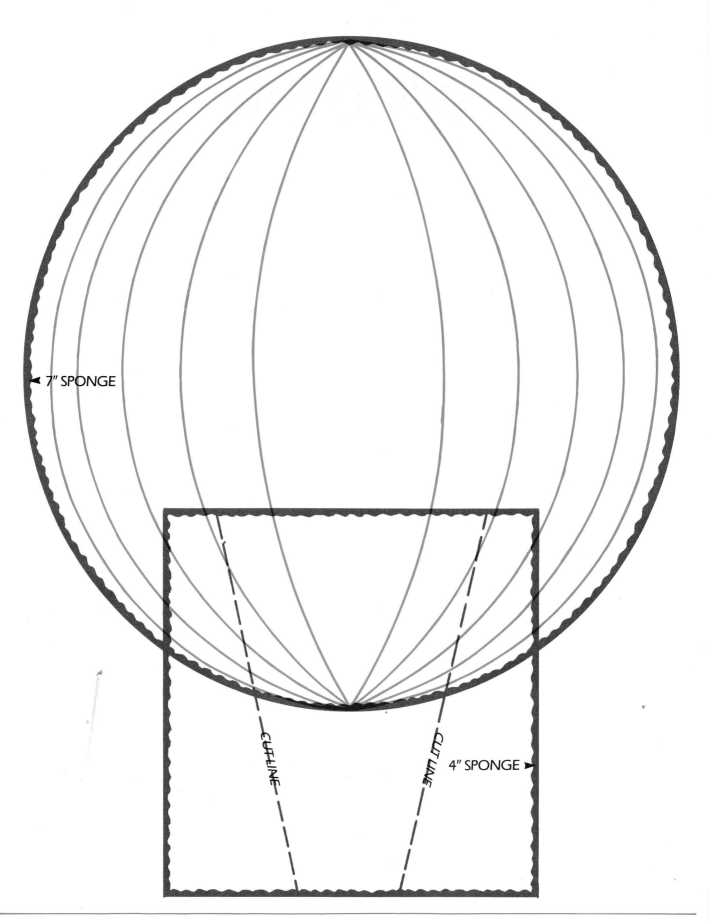

◄ 7" SPONGE

CUT LINE

CUT LINE

4" SPONGE ►

BARBIE

Cake Requirements

8″ square sponge
14″ round board
14″ round doyley
Buttercream

Edible colours
French pink – Green

Royal icing
Sleeping baby
Sugar paste

1. Cut sponge, as shown.

2. Slice off-cut into two pieces to form the headboard and pillow (trimming to the length required).

3. Slice, fill and cover bed with buttercream and then cover with sugar paste. Cover headboard with buttercream and then sugar paste. Place on doyley and board.

4. Cut the pillow into two pieces and shape each piece into an oval. Cover each oval with buttercream and then sugar paste. Crimp pillow edges (see page 10).

5. Place pillows on bed. Decorate each pillow with piped royal icing, then position baby as shown.

6. Roll out, cut and place a sugar paste cover over the baby's body and bed top. Make and fix a sugar paste frill around edges of the bed cover.

7. Pipe royal icing shells around cover and then decorate cover with piped royal icing and inscription of choice.

8. Make and place a sugar paste mat on the doyley and decorate with royal icing motifs and bootees (see page 9).

86

Before commencing any work on this page, please read the whole sequence of instructions and ensure the proper materials and equipment are to hand, as well as sufficient time to complete the cake. Additional information can be found on pages 4-11 (Index on page 120).

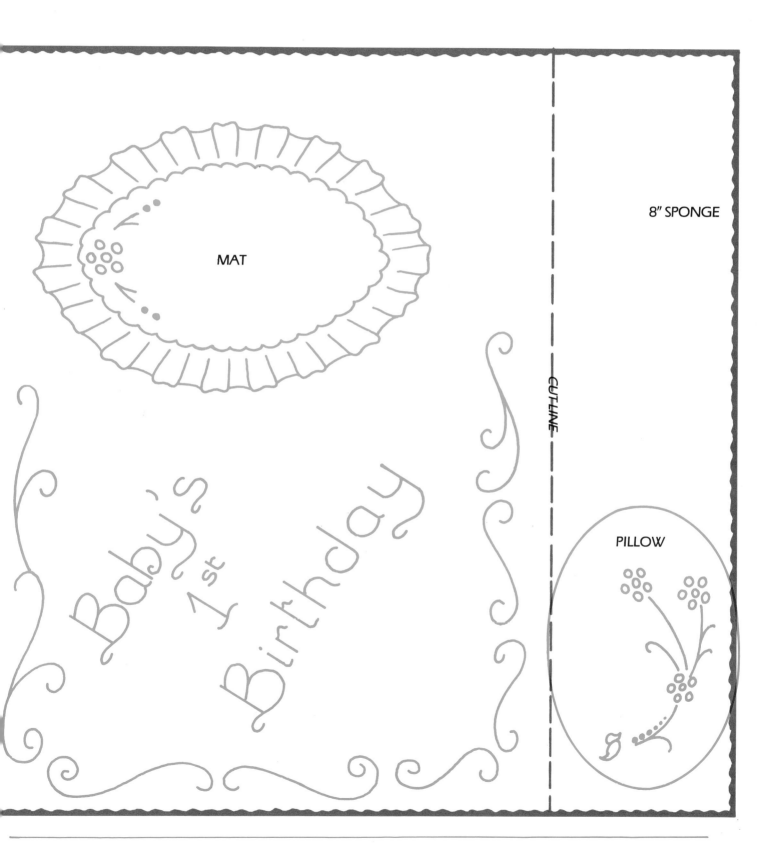

MAT

8" SPONGE

CUT LINE

Baby's 1st Birthday

PILLOW

JASON

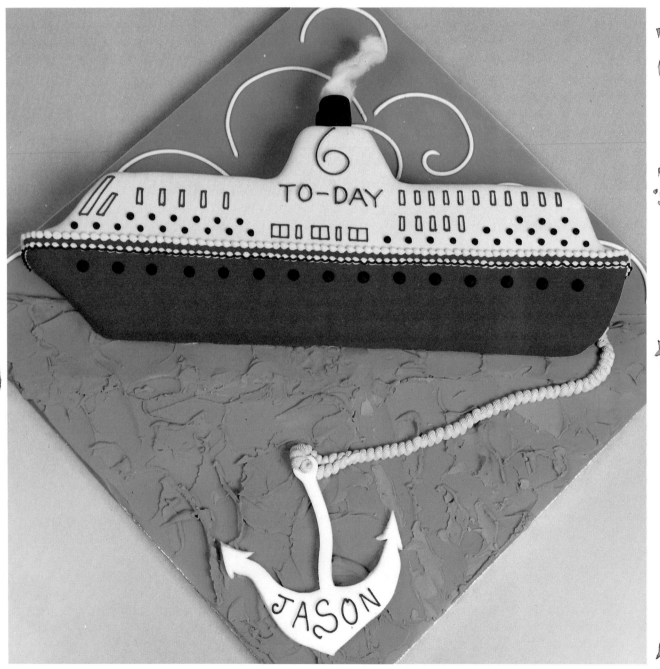

Cake Requirements

Two × 7" square sponges
14" square board
Buttercream

Edible colours
Black – Blue – Brown – Cream – Green – Red – Yellow

Royal icing
Sugar paste

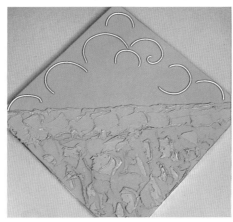

1. Cover board with sugar paste and royal icing to represent the sky and sea. Then pipe royal icing lines to form clouds.

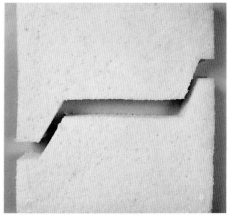

2. Place one sponge on top of the other and cut to the shape shown. Upturn top pieces and place beside the bottom pieces to form liner. Trim bow and stern.

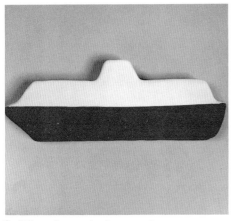

3. Fill and coat the liner with buttercream and then cover with two colours of sugar paste.

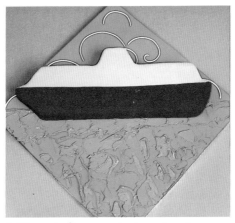

4. Place the liner on the board in the position shown.

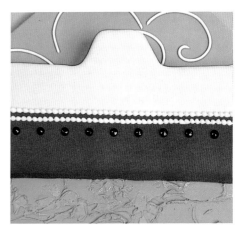

5. Pipe royal icing shells and bulbs along the centre of the liner.

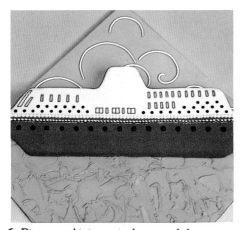

6. Pipe royal icing windows and doors on the liner's superstructure.

7. Mould and fix a sugar paste funnel and then add cotton wool to form smoke. Pipe royal icing "age" in position shown.

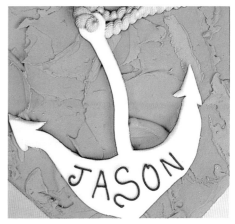

8. Roll out, cut and fix a sugar paste anchor and pipe royal icing rope and name of choice.

Before commencing any work on this page, please read the whole sequence of instructions and ensure the proper materials and equipment are to hand, as well as sufficient time to complete the cake. Additional information can be found on pages 4-11 (Index on page 120).

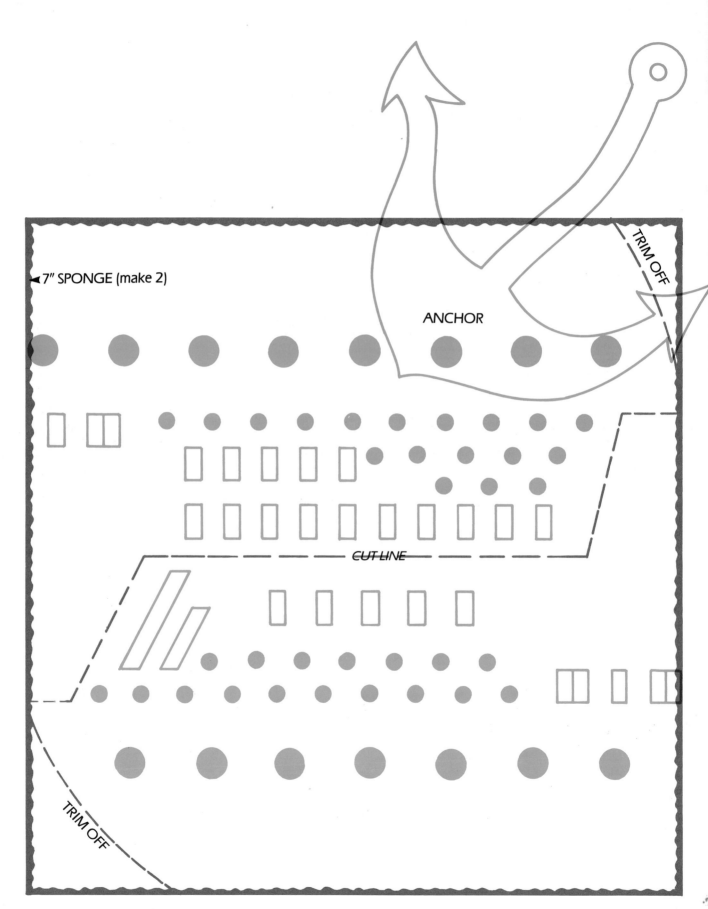

◄ 7" SPONGE (make 2)

ANCHOR

TRIM OFF

CUT LINE

TRIM OFF

PENNY

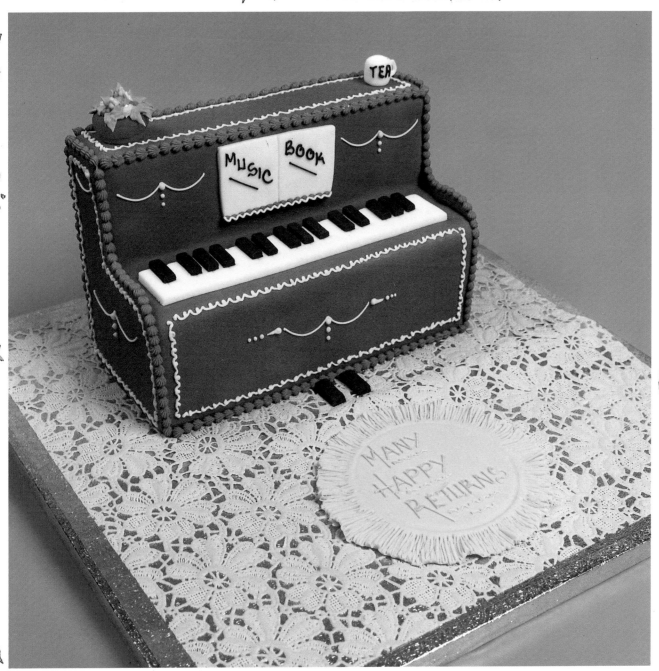

Cake Requirements

8″ square sponge
12″ square board
12″ square doyley
Buttercream

Edible colours
Black – Brown – Cream – Green – Orange

Royal icing
Sugar paste

1. Cut sponge as shown. Sandwich pieces together with buttercream in an upright position.

2. Cover the sponge in buttercream and then sugar paste to form a piano. Place on doyley and board.

3. Pipe royal icing shells around the piano's edges.

4. Roll out, cut and fix a sugar paste keyboard.

5. Roll out, cut and fix a sugar paste music book. Pipe royal icing words, lines and shells, as shown.

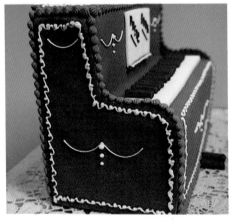

6. Decorate piano with piped royal icing, as indicated.

7. Roll out, cut and fix a sugar paste bowl to the piano top. Pipe royal icing leaves and flowers, as shown.

8. Roll out, cut and place a sugar paste mat on the doyley and decorate mat with piped royal icing.

Before commencing any work on this page, please read the whole sequence of instructions and ensure the proper materials and equipment are to hand, as well as sufficient time to complete the cake. Additional information can be found on pages 4-11 (Index on page 120).

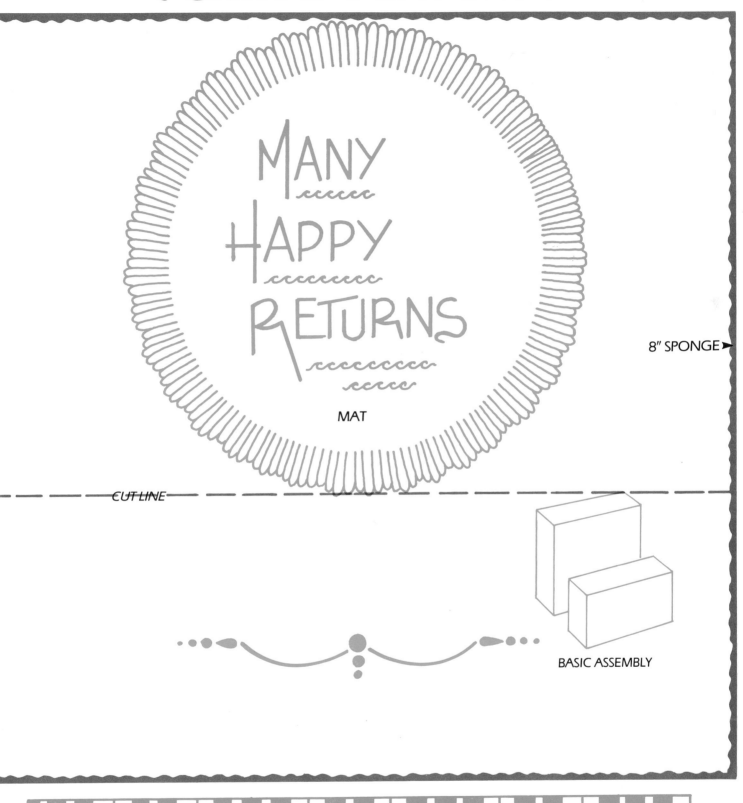

MANY HAPPY RETURNS

MAT

8" SPONGE ►

CUT LINE

BASIC ASSEMBLY

KEYBOARD

ANDY

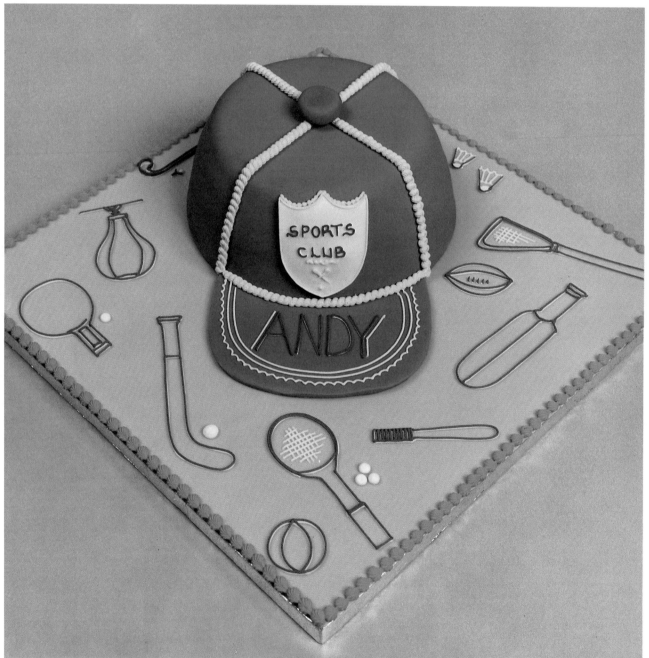

Cake Requirements

°Sponge baked in 2pt pudding basin
12″ square board
Buttercream

Edible colours
Blue – Brown – Cream – Green – Red

Royal icing
Sugar paste

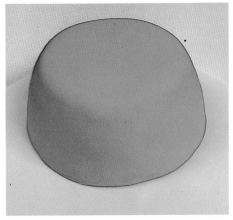

1. Remove the dome part of the sponge to achieve shape shown. Slice, fill and cover sponge with buttercream and then cover with sugar paste.

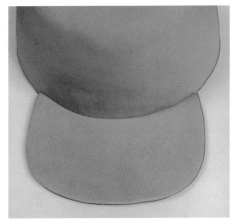

2. Place sponge on board coated with sugar paste. Roll out, cut and fix a sugar paste peak.

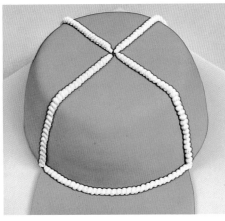

3. Pipe royal icing rope lines on cap, as shown. Mould and fix a sugar paste cap button to centre of cap top.

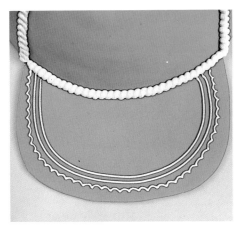

4. Pipe royal icing lines on peak, as shown.

5. Roll out, cut and fix a sugar paste cap badge. Decorate badge with piped royal icing.

6. Pipe royal icing name of choice on to the peak.

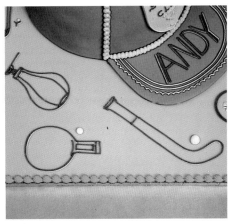

7. Pipe royal icing sports items on cake-board, as shown.

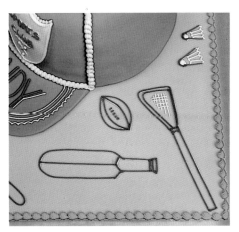

8. Pipe further royal icing sports items on cake-board and then shells around cake-board edge, as shown.

Before commencing any work on this page, please read the whole sequence of instructions and ensure the proper materials and equipment are to hand, as well as sufficient time to complete the cake. Additional information can be found on pages 4-11 (Index on page 120).

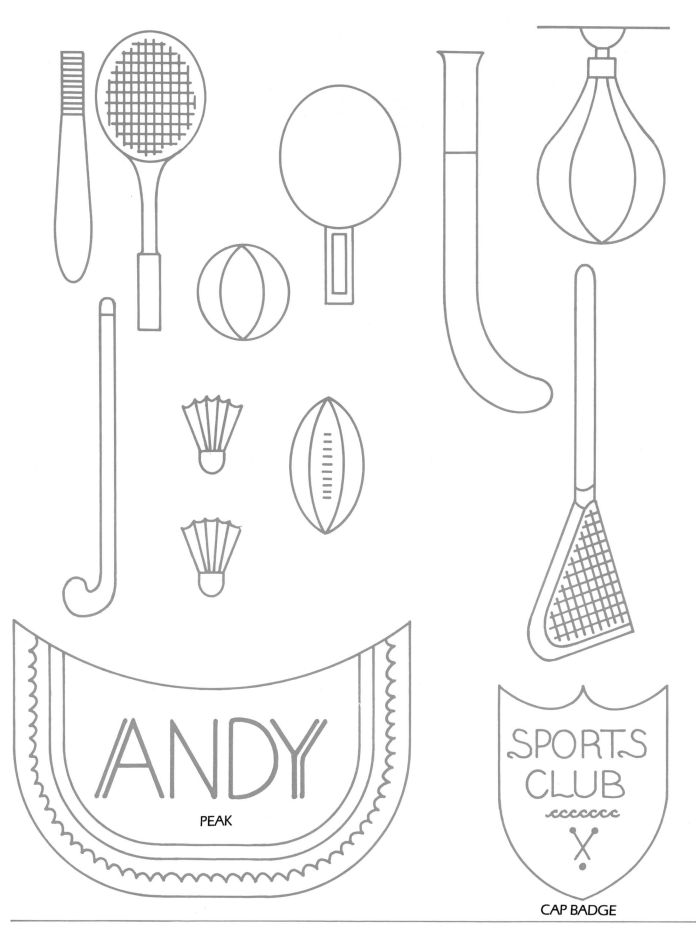

PEAK

ANDY

SPORTS CLUB

CAP BADGE

MANDY

Cake Requirements

8″ square sponge
12″ round board
12″ round doyley
Buttercream

Edible colours
Black – Blue – Brown – Green – Red – Yellow

Royal icing
Sugar paste

1. Slice, fill and cover the sponge with buttercream and then cover with sugar paste. Place on doyley and board.

2. Roll out, cut and fix the sugar paste day section of the calendar. Pipe the days in royal icing, as shown.

3. Pipe royal icing lines and numbers and highlight the birthday date.

4. Pipe the relevant birthday month in royal icing..

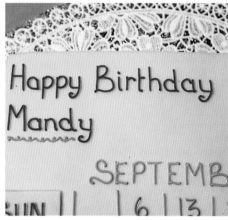

5. Pipe royal icing inscription of choice.

6. Decorate the calendar with piped royal icing floral motif and love birds.

7. Roll out, cut and fix sugar paste binder rings.

8. Roll out, cut and fix a sugar paste plaque. Then decorate the plaque with piped royal icing.

---

98 **Before commencing any work on this page, please read the whole sequence of instructions and ensure the proper materials and equipment are to hand, as well as sufficient time to complete the cake. Additional information can be found on pages 4-11 (Index on page 120).**

Happy Birthday
Mandy

8" SPONGE ►

SEPTEMBER

SUN		6	13	20	27
MON		7	14	21	28
TUES	1	8	15	22	29
WED	2	9	16	23	30
THURS	3	10	17	24	
FRI	4	11	18	25	
SAT	5	12	19	26	

ROCKY

Cake Requirements

Two × 8″ round sponges
12″ round board
Buttercream

Edible colours
*Black – Blue – Brown – Green – Orange
– Violet – Yellow*

Royal icing
Sugar paste

1. Sandwich sponges together with filling of choice, then cover side with buttercream and sugar paste. Place on board.

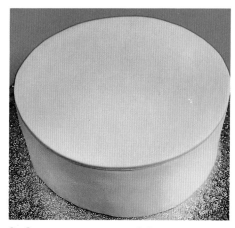

2. Cover sponge top with buttercream and sugar paste to form a drum.

3. Roll out, cut and fix sugar paste edging strips to the top and base.

4. Cut out and fix various sugar paste designs to the drum's side.

5. Roll out, cut and fix sugar paste tension cables around drum.

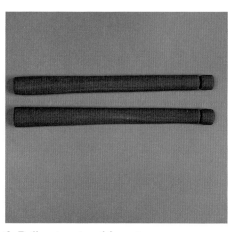

6. Roll out, cut and form two sugar paste drum sticks. Leave until dry.

7. Pipe royal icing inscription of choice and musical notes on drum top.

8. Place drum sticks in the position shown.

NOTE: Chocolate coated finger biscuits may be substituted for the sugar paste tension cables (in picture No. 5.) and drum sticks (in picture No.6).

Before commencing any work on this page, please read the whole sequence of instructions and ensure the proper materials and equipment are to hand, as well as sufficient time to complete the cake. Additional information can be found on pages 4-11 (Index on page 120).

SWEETIE

Cake Requirements

8″ square sponge
14″ round board
14″ round doyley
Buttercream

Edible colours
Black – Brown – Green – Pink – Violet – Yellow

Royal icing
Sugar paste

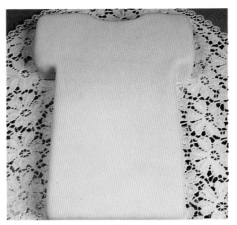

1. Cut sponge to the shapes shown. Remove the small off-cut and place the right-hand piece to the top of the sponge to form a T-shirt.

2. Slice, fill and cover the sponge with buttercream and then cover with sugar paste. Place on doyley and board.

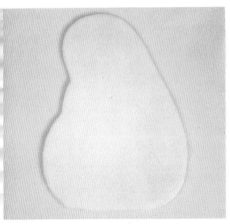

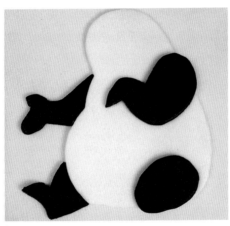

3. Roll out, cut and fix a sugar paste panda body to the T-shirt.

4. Roll out, cut and fix sugar paste arms and legs.

5. Roll out, cut and fix sugar paste ears, eyes and nose.

6. Roll out, cut and fix sugar paste feet. Pipe royal icing lines, dots, etc., to complete the panda – and then pipe royal icing bamboo shoots.

7. Roll out, cut and fix sugar paste strips to the T-shirt.

8. Pipe royal icing inscription of choice.

Before commencing any work on this page, please read the whole sequence of instructions and ensure the proper materials and equipment are to hand, as well as sufficient time to complete the cake. Additional information can be found on pages 4-11 (Index on page 120).

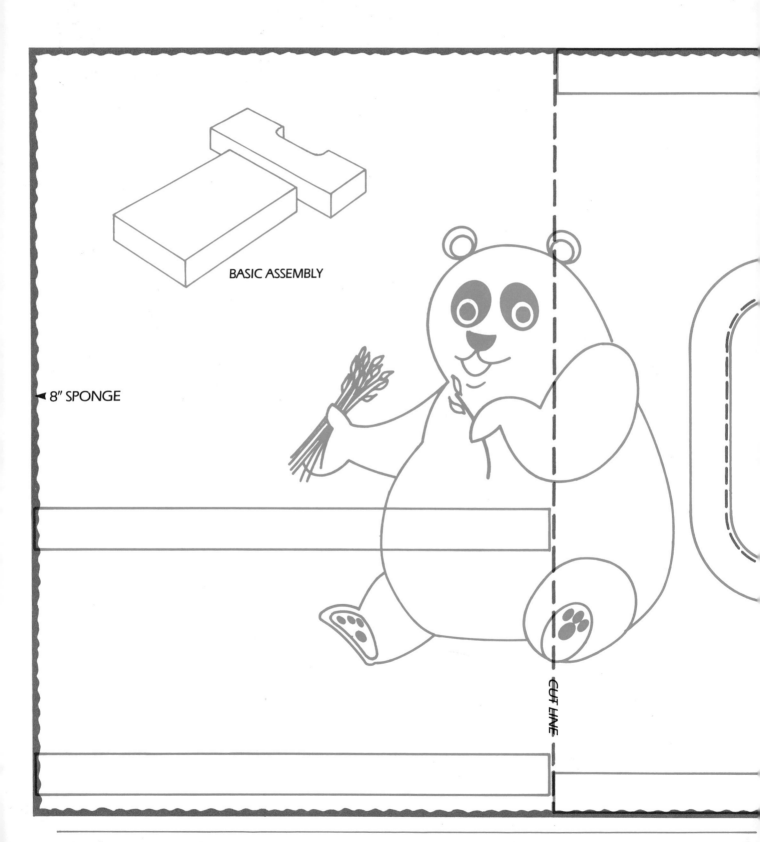

BASIC ASSEMBLY

◄ 8" SPONGE

CUT LINE

BARRY

Cake Requirements

8″ square sponge
14″ round board
Buttercream

Edible colours
Black – Blue – Green – Red – Yellow

Sugar paste
Royal icing

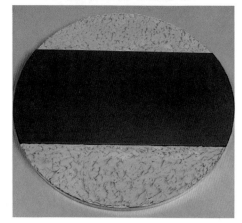

1. Roll out, cut and fix a sugar paste runway across the centre of the board. Stipple (see p.9) remainder of board with royal icing.

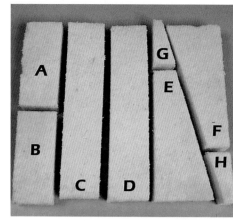

2. Cut sponge to the shapes shown.

3. Sandwich sponge pieces 'A', 'B', 'C' and 'D' with buttercream and trim to form plane's fuselage. Use trimmings to form tail.

4. Cover fuselage with buttercream and then sugar paste. Place on runway.

5. Cover tail and wing pieces 'E', 'F', 'G' and 'H' with buttercream and then sugar paste. Fix all pieces to fuselage.

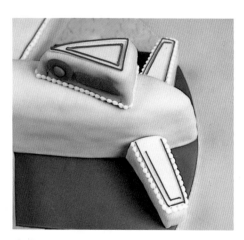

6. Decorate tail with sugar paste pieces and piped royal icing.

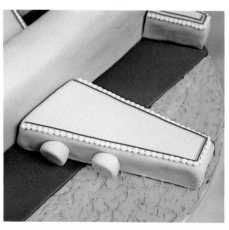

7. Decorate wings with sugar paste and piped royal icing.

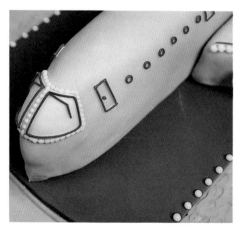

8. Pipe royal icing windows, doors and runway lights, then inscription of choice.

Before commencing any work on this page, please read the whole sequence of instructions and ensure the proper materials and equipment are to hand, as well as sufficient time to complete the cake. Additional information can be found on pages 4-11 (Index on page 120).

★★★★★★★★★★★★★★ BARRY'S TEMPLATE ★★★★★★★★★★★★★★★★

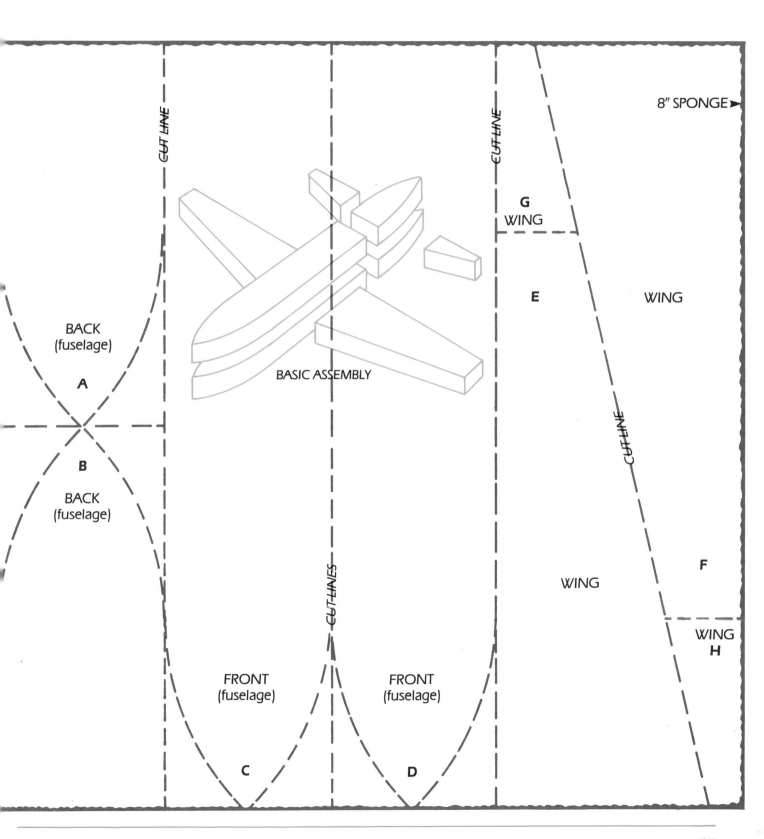

8" SPONGE ▶

CUT LINE

G
WING

CUT LINE

BASIC ASSEMBLY

E

WING

BACK
(fuselage)

A

WING

B

CUT LINE

BACK
(fuselage)

F

WING

WING
H

CUT-LINES

FRONT
(fuselage)

C

FRONT
(fuselage)

D

COOKIE

Cake Requirements

6″ round sponge
5″ square sponge
12″ × 14″ board
Buttercream

Edible colours
*Black – Blue – Brown – French pink –
Green – Red*

Royal icing
Sugar paste

1. Cut, slice and fill sponges with buttercream. Place off-cut to top of square cake to form chef's hat.

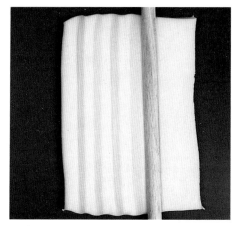

2. Roll out sugar paste and press with a dowel to form chef's hat crinkles.

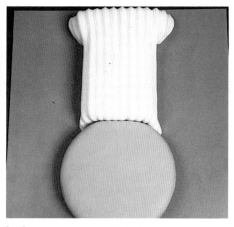

3. Cover sponge with buttercream and then cover chef's hat with prepared sugar paste. Cover round sponge with sugar paste and place sponges on board.

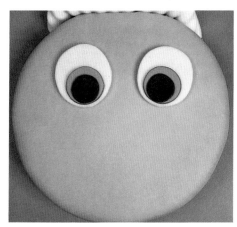

4. Roll out, cut and fix white, blue and black sugar paste discs to form chef's eyes.

5. Cut out and fix sugar paste discs and join with a royal icing piped line. Mould and fix a sugar paste nose.

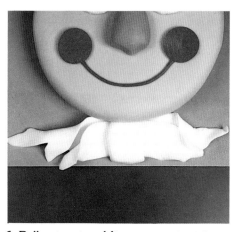

6. Roll out, cut and fix sugar paste strips to form a neck band.

7. Roll out, cut and fix a sugar paste beard. Mould and place a sugar paste rolling pin and spoon on the board.

8. Roll out and cut a sugar paste menu card, then decorate with royal icing, as shown. Place in position when dry.

Before commencing any work on this page, please read the whole sequence of instructions and ensure the proper materials and equipment are to hand, as well as sufficient time to complete the cake. Additional information can be found on pages 4-11 (Index on page 120).

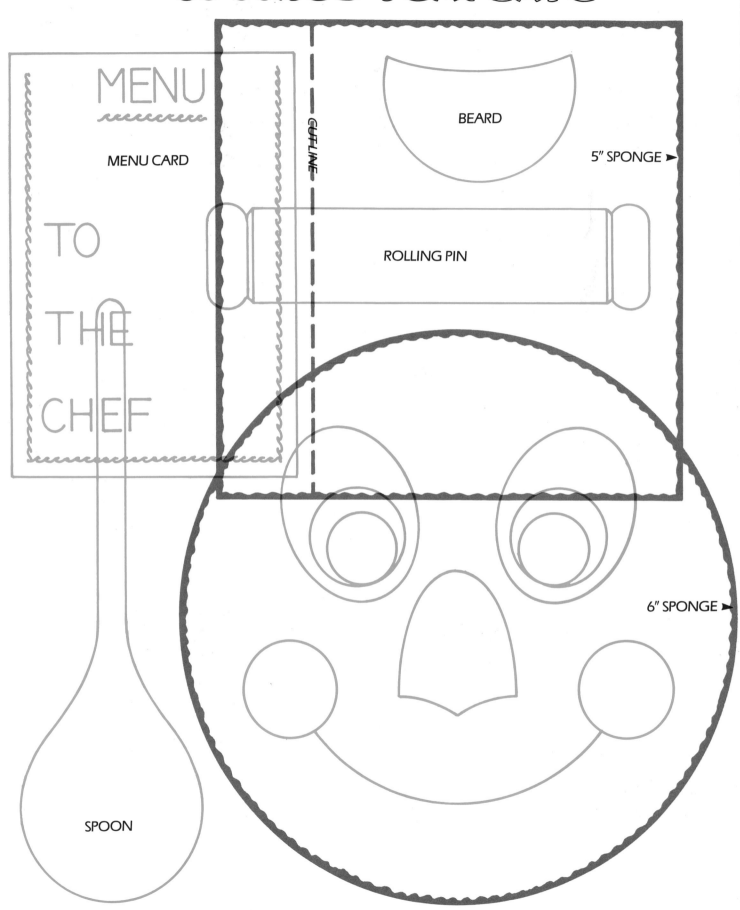

MENU

MENU CARD

TO

THE

CHEF

BEARD

5" SPONGE ►

CUTLINE

ROLLING PIN

6" SPONGE ►

SPOON

SANDIE

SPORT

GOOD
LUCK

Cake Requirements

8″ square sponge
12″ round board
12″ round doyley
Buttercream

Edible colours
Black – Blue – Brown – Green – Orange – Red – Yellow

Royal icing
Sugar paste

1. Cut sponge into three and sandwich together with filling of choice. Cover with buttercream.

2. Cover sponge with sugar paste to form sports bag and then place on doyley and board.

3. Cut, mark and fix sugar paste to form zips. Pipe royal icing stitching lines.

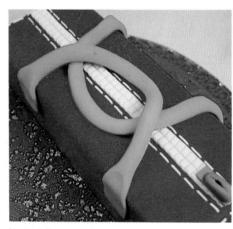

4. Roll out and fix sugar paste handles.

5. Pipe royal icing stitching at each end of bag.

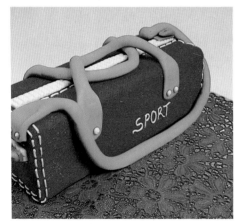

6. Roll out and fix sugar paste shoulder strap. Pipe royal icing rivets on handles and strap, then pipe the word "SPORT".

7. Roll out and cut sugar paste socks, shorts and towel. Pipe royal icing lines on socks and shorts.

8. Pipe inscription of choice in royal icing on to the towel.

Before commencing any work on this page, please read the whole sequence of instructions and ensure the proper materials and equipment are to hand, as well as sufficient time to complete the cake. Additional information can be found on pages 4-11 (Index on page 120).

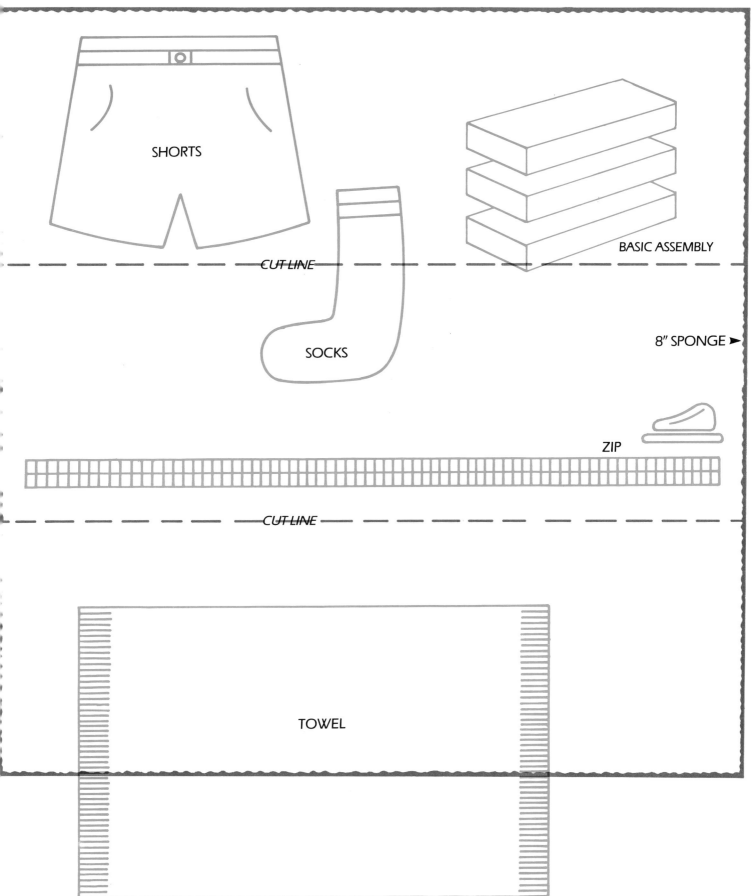

SHORTS

BASIC ASSEMBLY

CUT LINE

SOCKS

8" SPONGE ►

ZIP

CUT LINE

TOWEL

FREDDIE

Cake Requirements

8″ square sponge
14″ round board
14″ round doyley
Buttercream

Edible colours
Black – Blue – Orange – Red – Yellow

Royal icing
Sugar paste

1. Cut sponge to the shapes shown.

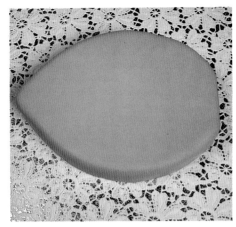

2. Slice, fill and cover the centre sponge with buttercream and then cover with sugar paste. Place on doyley and board.

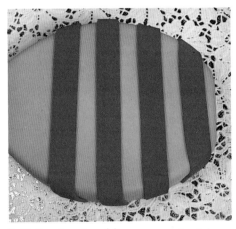

3. Roll out, cut and fix sugar paste strips to the fish's body.

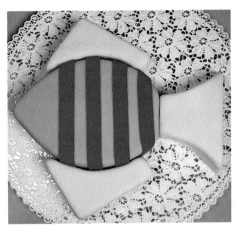

4. Join the two small sponge off-cuts to form a tail. Slice, fill and cover the tail and fins with buttercream and then sugar paste.

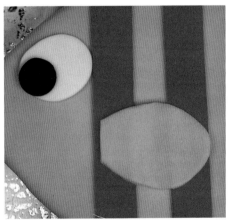

5. Join fish tail and fins to the body. Roll out, cut and fix sugar paste eye ball, eye and side fin.

6. Decorate fish head with piped royal icing.

7. Pipe royal icing lines on fins and tail.

8. Roll out, cut and fix a sugar paste baby fish and decorate with piped royal icing. Roll out, cut and fix sugar paste bubbles.

Before commencing any work on this page, please read the whole sequence of instructions and ensure the proper materials and equipment are to hand, as well as sufficient time to complete the cake. Additional information can be found on pages 4-11 (Index on page 120).

FREDDIE'S TEMPLATE

BUBBLES

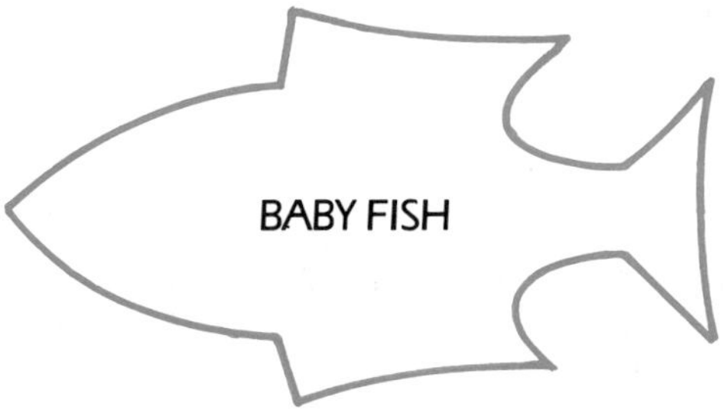

BABY FISH

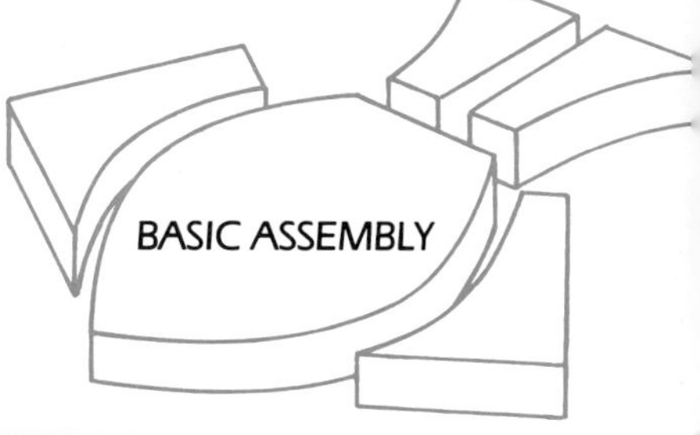

BASIC ASSEMBLY

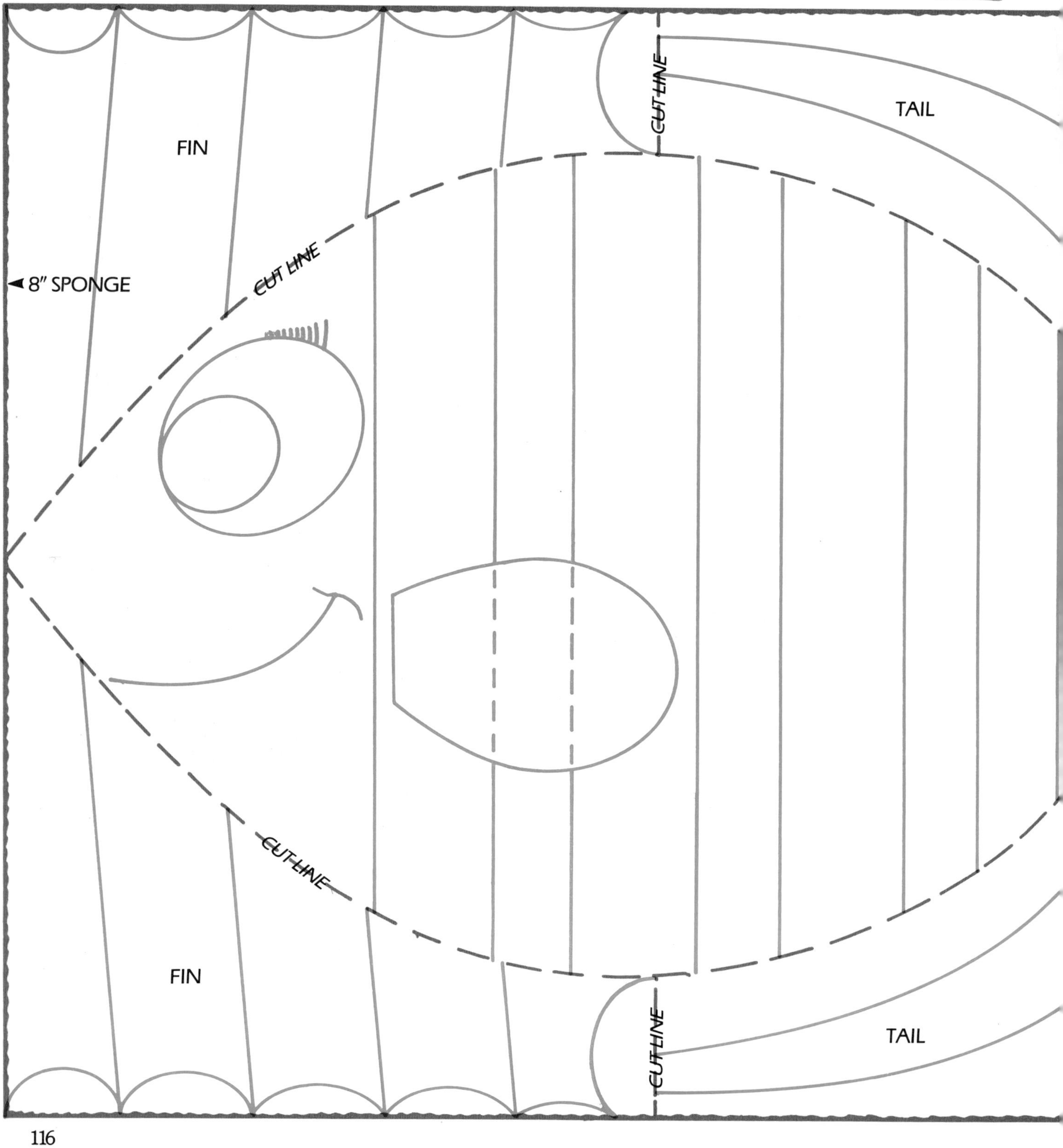

TAIL

FIN

CUT LINE

◀ 8" SPONGE

CUT LINE

CUT LINE

FIN

CUT LINE

TAIL

FROSTIE

Cake Requirements

4″ and 8″ round sponges
14″ round board
16″ round doyley
Buttercream

Edible colours
Black – Blue – Christmas Red – Cream – Green – Moss Green – Orange

Royal icing
Sugar paste

1. Cut sponges to the shape shown and use off-cuts to make hat. Slice each piece and fill with buttercream.

2. Cover with buttercream and then with sugar paste. Place snowman on doyley and cake-board.

3. Roll out, cut and fix sugar paste eyes and nose.

4. Pipe royal icing dots and lines to form features shown.

5. Roll out, cut and fix sugar paste scarf and buttons.

6. Roll out, cut and fix sugar paste hatband and holly leaves. Mould and fix sugar paste berries. Pipe royal icing snow and icicles.

7. Roll out, cut and fix sugar paste discs to form snowflakes.

8. Pipe "Christmas", as shown, with royal icing.

Before commencing any work on this page, please read the whole sequence of instructions and ensure the proper materials and equipment are to hand, as well as sufficient time to complete the cake. Additional information can be found on pages 4-11 (Index on page 120).

FROSTIE'S TEMPLATE ★★★★★★★★★★★★★★★★★

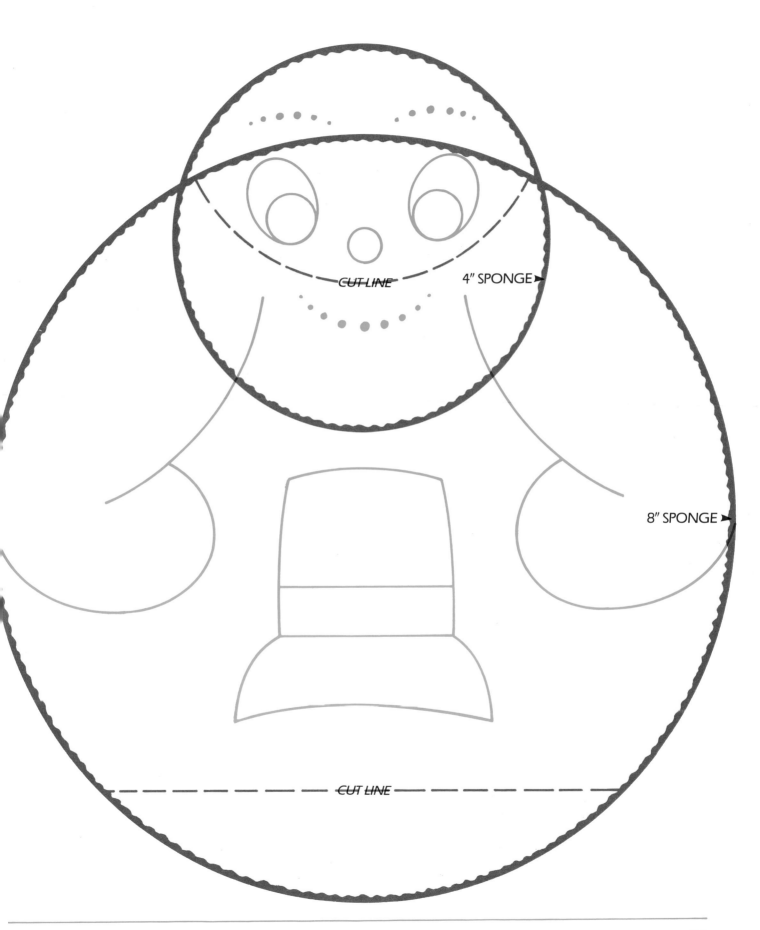

CUT LINE

4" SPONGE ▶

8" SPONGE ▶

CUT LINE

✶✶✶✶✶✶✶✶✶✶✶ INDEX AND GLOSSARY ✶✶✶✶✶✶✶✶✶✶✶

*Mary Ford thanks you for buying this book
and hopes it will give you much pleasure.*